Dreams My Mother Taught Me

Lessons in Lucid Dreaming from Beyond the Grave

Dreams My Mother Taught Me

Lessons in Lucid Dreaming from Beyond the Grave

Melinda Powell

First published in the United Kingdom by
Archive Publishing
Shaftesbury, Dorset, England

www.archivepublishing.co.uk

Designed at Archive Publishing by Ian Thorp MA

10 9 8 7 6 5 4 3 2 1

Copyright © 2025 Archive Publishing
Text Copyright © Melinda Powell, 2025

Melinda Powell asserts the moral right to be
identified as the author of this work in accordance with the
Copyright, Design and Patents Act, 1988.

The term Lucid Surrender ™ is a registered trademark of Melinda Powell.

This book is copyright under the Berne Convention.
No reproduction without the prior permission of the publisher.
All rights reserved.

A CIP catalogue record for this book is available from The British Library.

ISBN 978-1-906289-67-6 (Paperback)
ISBN 978-1-906289-77-5 (Ebook/Kindle)

Cover art and Parts I–IV title page artwork: © Eri Griffin Illustrations

The author and publisher shall have no liability or responsibility to any person or entity regarding any loss, damage or injury incurred, or alleged to have incurred, directly or indirectly, by the information contained in this book.

DEDICATION

*To Margaret,
pearl of great price*

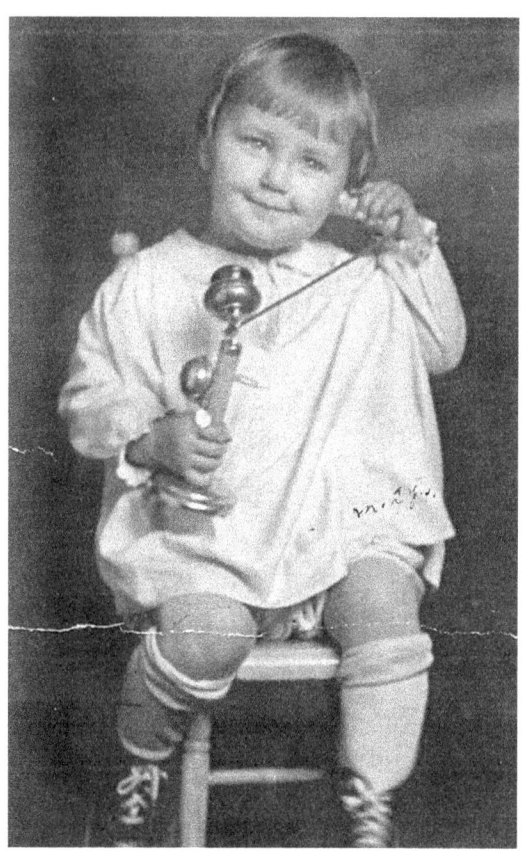

Margaret Elizabeth Williams

Hello Central, give me Heaven,
For I know my mother's there.
And you will find her with the angels,
Over on the golden stair.

— From a song by Charles K. Harris (1901)

Contents

Acknowledgements   13
Foreword by Jeanne Van Bronkhurst, MA, MSW   15
Note to the Reader   17
Prologue: The End is in the Beginning   21

Part One
Lessons in Surrender

Cutting the Cord   29
My Mother's Gifts   35
The Dark Womb of Creation   41
Back Home Again   47
Mirroring Soul   59
The Way to Blue   65

Part Two
Lessons in Light

The Holy of Holies   73
Trust in Light and Love   79
The Body of Light   85
Celestial Cities   91
Gifts of the Spirit   97

Part Three
Lessons in Grace

One More	105
New Light	117
Enveloped in Love	121
Where Heaven and Earth Touch	127
Coming Home	141

Part Four
Lessons in Life & Beyond

The Eternal Well of Living Light	149
The Refining Fire of Spirit	153
Living Waters	159
The Healing Power of Lucidity	165
Wearing Soul on the Outside	171
List of Dreams	177
Treasured Family Memories	179
Notes	183

Acknowledgements

One winter's night, shortly after I started this book, my mother, who had passed away twenty-one years before, appeared in a dream, sitting down in the chair next to my writing desk. She looked on silently and supportively as I wrote, tilting her head slightly as she read along and nodding approvingly, a Mona Lisa smile on her lips.

In the dream, I was sufficiently lucid to know that she had already passed over and to wonder what she wanted me to write. I asked her to look at me, and when she did, a flood of emotion awakened me from sleep. Initially, I felt frustrated with myself for being unable to contain the strong feelings that roused me, but then it occurred to me that my mother had given me exactly what was needed — the knowledge that she was watching on and was pleased that I would be writing about our encounters together in dream lucidity.

Having now completed *Dreams My Mother Taught Me: Lessons in Lucid Dreaming from Beyond the Grave*, I thank her for the life she gave me and the continued light of her presence in my lucid dreams. It's good to know that her loving guidance will now reach others through these pages.

When I reviewed the entire dream cycle with my husband, Andrew, and its import for my mother's healing and mine, it struck me that not only am I, as a therapist and lucid dreamer, uniquely placed to write this book but also that Andrew, with his understanding of transpersonal psychotherapy has been wonderfully suited to help me edit the manuscript.

In that same moment of reflection, there flashed before my eyes a vision of my mother, smiling the same beatific smile that had shone from her face in the moments before her death. She had been lying motionless in a morphine induced coma when she suddenly sat up in bed, looking bright and beautiful, her eyes falling directly on my brother, Steve, her first-born, on the bed next to her. Now, she was smiling in turn upon Andrew and me as if sharing in our mutual pleasure and bestowing a blessing. Her expression spoke of the circle of joy that had been completed in her, and our, lives.

A few years before, Andrew and I had placed my mother's ashes amidst the roots of a rose bush that we planted in our garden. Looking out from the kitchen window on a summer's morn, I can see a cluster of yellow roses — my mother's favorite color — shining brightly in the sun, reminding me of the love she and I had re-discovered in lucidity.

There was a time when I could never have imagined my mother and I sharing in the experiences recorded here. Nor could I have foreseen that I would be able to reflect on them with a man who, like me, trusts that love and learning continue beyond the grave. Thank you, Andrew, for all the help you have given me in writing this book so dear to my heart.

Likewise, my thanks to you, the reader, for joining me on this journey of discovery.

Foreword

I become lucid and say, "I know I'm dreaming, Lord, if you want to, come for me." As I do so, the dreamscape gives way to the Black Light, where a current of wind carries my soul very fast for a great distance. Repeating a sacred song helps me to keep focused.

With these words, author Melinda Powell launches the reader into realms of intense beauty, through spiritually powerful transcendent lucid dreams These transcendent experiences haven't asked her to transcend her own life, however, but to deepen it. She writes of how this series of lucid dreams helped her reconcile with the past and to move forward in life.

In this collection of dreams, Melinda's mother returns after her death to help Melinda on her own path. "It seems to me now that my mother's mission in my lucid dreams was to help me re-establish trust in myself and in life…so that in waking life I could find that still center, a wellspring of love that is the soul's nature and purpose".

This is a book about love and forgiveness, and the power of extraordinary dreams to help us heal our most important relationships long after we have been separated by death. The narrative skillfully weaves back and forth between dream and memory, tugging at Melinda's relationship with each parent and with her dream figures, using stories to illuminate their lives. All the while, her dreams hold her and challenge her, supporting her longing for reconciliation. They illuminate her life and call her into a loving embrace of the people who raised her.

Melinda's dreams bring healing personal memories and the deeper understanding of her mother and father as fallible human beings, beyond their roles as her parents. Her dreams allow her to appreciate and learn from her mother's life choices. And her trust in her dreams helps Melinda return to her father's side, home in time to be with him in his final days.

This is compassion and self-compassion. This is emotional growth and a spiritual deepening of Christianity's essence. It is beautiful and poetic and psychologically astute. She writes, "Much therapeutic work revolves around learning to regain a sense of trust in our own intuition and in life itself, a trust that may have been violated, whether intentionally or not, by those we originally viewed with childlike faith, whether our parents, caregivers, or the wider world." If this is so, and I have every reason to believe it is so, then Melinda's dreams have given her a very rich life indeed. Her dreams have enriched my life as well, and I believe they will invite every reader into a new relationship with their own dreams, with their own possibilities.

Jeanne Van Bronkhurst, MA, MSW, (Canada)
Former hospice social worker and author of *Dreams at the Threshold: Guidance, Comfort and Healing at the End of Life* (2015), and *Premonitions in Daily life* (2013).

Note to the Reader

On my thirty-eighth birthday, my mother, Margaret, died, crossing over with her now adult children at her bedside. Even now, years on, whenever I see mothers and daughters conversing intimately, my heart quietly grieves. Whoever first said, "We're born alone, and we die alone" misses the point — the woman who bore you knows that she was with you on the day you were born!

After my mother's death, I felt both bereft and fortunate to have been with her in the months before she died of cancer. Her death felt doubly hard because I had lived abroad for many years. When I left the United States for Europe at twenty-five, she cried, "You will never come back!" Her words proved prophetic, for although I returned home often for visits, I settled in England.

If you have loved and lost your mother, you will have a sense of grief personal to you, one that resurfaces when you suddenly have the urge to talk with her or give her a hug. I call those unexpected emotional implosions "love-bombs", when deep memories and feelings silently burst the heart wide open.

Like me, you may wish you had got on better with your mother and had known her more as a person in her own right. It can be all the harder to accept the loss if she has left without saying "I love you", or without your having the chance to say the same. There may not have been time to ask for mutual forgiveness and understanding, leaving you both with many unanswered "Whys?".

Whether or not your mother has passed to the "other side", I present you, the reader, with a hope — that love continues beyond the grave. Even when the human relationship has been fraught, the departed soul, free from the adversities of life, will so often seek to love and make amends.

I share here the story of how my relationship with my mother deepened after her death as she initiated me into lucid dreaming. To do so, I'll draw on several key dreams that began a month after she died, and which have continued throughout the years.

It took me some time to understand fully what her presence in my lucid dreams signified. This realization was heightened five years on from her passing, when I had a lucid dream that I call "The Letter from Beyond the Veil", in which she communicated to me directly about her on-going role in my life:

> *My mother appears and hands me a letter that she clearly had wanted to give me before she died in waking life. She has written in pink ink on fine white parchment edged in the same soft rosy hue. I feel the love and attention given to its making. I can read this letter quite clearly. It says, "I am going before you, so you needn't fear. All in this life, I will help make new. And I will do what I could not do for you here [on Earth]. You only need to watch the future unfold." These words comfort me.*

Little did I know then how much my life would be changing in the years following this dream. At difficult times, I returned to this letter for renewed encouragement and to gain confidence in the future.

Re-reading my mother's message, I notice that in most of the other dreams in which she has appeared, she has communicated wordlessly. Like a sybil, she speaks in meaningful signs and symbols, and even her written words often remain vague enough to be open to interpretation. In my dream lucidity, what has mattered most is the way in which her loving presence has guided me. This has made all the difference.

Some readers might say my visions of my mother are nothing more than a projection of my dreaming mind. Others might argue that from beyond the veil she truly appeared. But I sense both are true.

Either way, I hope that my own experience will speak to you in a personal way and that my sharing these dreams my mother taught me may reassure you that love never dies.

Prologue

The End is in the Beginning

Dying takes a good deal of energy. I learned this when I returned to the United States from Europe to care for my mother as she lay dying of cancer. Watching her waste away, I could see how dying consumed her. There was much she wanted to say, but she could only lift a trembling hand to gently touch a tendril of my long, curly hair.

I expressed myself mostly by tenderly bathing and feeding her. Once when I washed her, she said, "I never thought my daughter would clean under my flaccid breasts." I said it was okay; after all, she had cleaned me countless times when I was a baby. We both wanted to say, "Yes, but then there was joy." In the hospital, during those long weeks when the doctors finally discovered her cancer, she said to me, "I'm so glad that I had you, even though I hadn't planned to have another baby." Another time she remarked, "For the first time in my life, I'm glad you don't have children," meaning I was free to care for her.

Early in her thirty-eighth year, unaware that she was pregnant with me, my mother had determined to leave my father. She arranged a meeting with the minister at our Baptist church and told him, "I don't want that man touching me and I don't want to bear any more of his children." She'd already had my brothers, aged nine and seven, and had miscarried two boys, one nearly full-term. The minister looked at an invisible point across the room and told her it was a wife's duty to stay with her husband no matter what — not even his temper or violent moods were reasons for leaving, such was the oath she made before God.

I privately wondered if Mom ever thought that God hadn't honored His side of the bargain. However, she didn't seem able or willing to talk about existential questions before her death. Dying demanded all her concentration.

Three weeks after her meeting with the minister, my mother had a positive pregnancy test and ended up staying married to Dad for forty-nine years in all, passing away a few months before their fiftieth anniversary. During her hospital stay, Dad told each new nurse caring for her, "You know, my wife was a nurse. We met in the hospital where she was working. She told me she wouldn't date a patient. That was forty-nine years ago!" The nurses looked at Dad, with his white teeth and dark tan, still going strong at seventy-two, and would smile conspiratorially. Mom managed a weak smile too, closed her eyes and sighed, "Does he always have to tell that story?"

Over the years, she had talked now and again about leaving Dad. It never seemed to be a definite plan, more a way to vent her frustrations. As the anniversaries added up, she talked about why she *hadn't* left Dad. Only many decades later could I acknowledge that, "for better or worse", she hadn't been able to protect us children — or herself — from his outbursts of wrath.

Refusing chemotherapy and accepting her terminal diagnosis, Mom finally "left" Dad. Her "last wish" was to die in North Carolina, at the home of my brother Carey, surrounded by beauty and peace. Ironically, my parents had planned to move to North Carolina from California later that same year. They'd bought a townhouse near Carey's family and were waiting for the construction to be completed in the autumn, after my father, who was a dentist for forty-seven years, retired. My mother, though, would never see the finished home before her death.

When my parents could no longer make love because the tumor in my mother's bladder made having sex painful for her, the physical bond that had held them together broke. I knew Mom was serious in her determination to distance herself from him when she stopped asking what he'd had to eat and when she stopped worrying about his dirty laundry.

Dad spent time sitting with her in hospital, but he couldn't bear seeing her wither away racked by dry heaves and pain. By this time, Mom, at five feet seven inches tall, weighed less than the one-hundred-pound backpacks Dad used to carry on hiking trips. She would say, "Walt, don't just sit there and stare at me with those sad eyes."

I asked her if she and Dad had talked things over. She said, "I asked him what he thought about the doctors' diagnosis, and he said, "They're all full of shit." Dad kept hoping that if the doctors tinkered with Mom enough, she'd be fixed, as if her body were like one of the many car engines he'd revived. He told her, "If you don't have chemo, you're going to die." Mom, who was lying on her bed, slowly raised her trembling hands, palms open, in an I'm-going-to-die-anyway gesture. Dad said to me, "You're married forty-nine years, and you get to thinking nothing can happen."

With the help of a family friend to whom our mom had been a second mother, my brother Carey arranged for Mom to fly first class from California, where my parents lived, to North Carolina, fulfilling one of her lifelong dreams. When I told her that her doctor had advised against traveling, she replied, "If I die, I die in first class," her deadpan humor showing signs of life. Carey asked Dad if he would be coming out to North Carolina to be with Mom, and Dad answered tangentially, "Well, son, I didn't go to my mom's funeral, and Margaret didn't go to her mom's funeral. We just don't like funerals." Dad had tentatively asked Mom, "Say Margaret, uh, you know, about your dying, you don't want a funeral, do you?" She replied with a definitive, "No," and added, "I want to be cremated."

We brought Mom home from hospital for a few days before the trip to North Carolina. Dad had a notary come to the house to witness her signing over her portion of the "estate". I happened to enter the dimly lit room just as Dad leaned over Mom in her bed to hand her a pen. The outlines of their bodies silhouetted in a shadow play against the half-opened slats in the blind alongside Mom's bed. I left the room silently and waited in the kitchen.

Once the notary had left, Dad came into the kitchen muttering *goddamns*. He leant over the documents spread out on the table, protesting that it was all too much, and sobbed. I patted his heaving shoulders and told him to go ahead and cry. I wanted to ask what the tears were saying.

In the end, I was the one who packed my mother's

belongings for the move to North Carolina. Although it was early June, Mom asked me to pack her winter clothes, ignoring the doctors' prognosis that she only had a short time to live. Crying softly, I collected her things. When I asked her if she ever felt like crying, she answered, "Sometimes."

She did cry, though, when she asked if I wanted to take her doll Honeybunch back to Europe with me. Honeybunch was the only doll that had ever mattered to me as a child, and I rarely played with her, except to brush her long, curly hair. She belonged to my mother and sat high up on her dresser. Her ringlets came from my grandmother, and the curls were still thick after sixty-six years.

These ringlets tell a story of love and loss. In 1936, when work was hard to come by, my mother's father went off to the Yukon in Alaska to search for gold. As money was short, Grandma cut her knee-length hair and sold it to buy each of her three daughters a doll for Christmas.

My mother always thought she'd have a little girl that looked like Honeybunch. That was to be me, though my curls were never so thick. So, when she asked if I wanted the doll, I took offense. How could I *not* want Honeybunch? She meant so much to us both. I started crying and told Mom that she'd surprised me. Mom started crying too and said, "It's just that when you left America, you left behind all the beautiful things you once wanted. And you never were one for dolls. I love you so much, I wouldn't say anything to hurt you." I sat down next to Mom and said, "Well, I guess I surprised you too." She replied, "You sure did."

While packing her things, I found signposts from her

life tucked behind the underwear and socks in her dresser drawers: letters yellow with age that she'd written to her dad when he was away in Alaska: a half-filled photograph album with black and white photographs of Mom, her sisters, and cousins in swimsuits on cold, pebbly Seattle beaches; her certificate of graduation from the School of Nursing at the University of Washington; the silver bracelet lined with molar-charms that Dad had made for her when he was a dental student during their courtship in San Francisco; the string of pearls from the time Dad was stationed in Okinawa, Japan, with the US air force; swatches of hair from my brothers' first haircuts; postcards I'd sent her from European cities; and all the empty bottles from the many prescriptions the urologist had given her for the pain he had long misdiagnosed as a kidney infection.

After the diagnosis of terminal cancer, my eldest brother, Steve, and I accompanied Mom on the long journey from California to Carey's home in North Carolina. On the way, she managed to look out of her window for a final view of the Sierra Nevada Mountains. We flew over Mount Whitney and then Death Valley: the highest and lowest points in the continental United States. Somehow that was fitting. She gazed weakly at the scene spread beneath her and sighed, "How beautiful."

My mother was to live for a few more months but that night when we finally got her into bed and Carey asked her how she felt, she replied, "I feel like I want to die." He teased tenderly, "You can die if you want to Mom, but why don't you take your medicine first?" That night was the only time in the short while remaining that she spoke to me about her past.

"You are wonderful kids, but I wasn't a wonderful wife."

"What do you mean?" I asked.

"I spent too much time with you kids and not enough with Dad."

"You loved each other in your own way," I offered.

"Boy, that's true," she affirmed, her head nodding forward in accord.

Part One

Lessons in Surrender

Cutting the Cord

On the day of my mother's death, when the undertakers came to take our mom to the funeral home, my brothers and I sat together in the kitchen, watching the gurney bearing her pass by through the adjacent sitting room.

As she was rolled out of my brother Carey's house, the weeks when she lay dying coalesced in my mind into a hasty, unspoken goodbye. With no ceremony to mark her passing, my brothers and I bought a few small antique vases from second-hand shops to house the remnants of her ashes, dividing up her remains, to be ceremonially spread as each of us wished.

Shortly thereafter, "Mom" and I flew back to London, where the spring had turned to late summer and once vibrant leaves had begun to look burnt by the sun. Upon entering my flat, I found a thrush dead on the balcony. Its lifeless form mirrored the loss of my mother, who could always "sing like a bird". For weeks, I felt struck down like that thrush, unable to cry or grieve for my mother until after the following dream:

I am walking in the neighborhood where my parents raised me but where newer, more expensive homes had been built in what had once been an orange grove.

A woman, with luminescent sky-blue skin, opens the front door to one of the new, freshly painted white houses and invites me in. I see that everything inside has a sky-blue hue, the walls, furniture, and objects.

She leads me to a room where my mother rests, sitting up in a bed with a blue bedspread over her legs. My mother looks radiant and joyful, surrounded by family members and friends who have died. They stand on either side of the bed in great numbers.

Becoming lucid enough to know that in this dream I see my mother in the world "beyond", I run up to her and place my head on her lap, crying out how much I love her and how sorry I am for whatever I may have done to hurt her. She pats me lovingly and patiently.

For the first time since her death, I begin to cry, and then I awake, still weeping.

This dream, which I called "The Blue Room", initiated my grieving process and gave me the chance to tell my mother what I had wanted to say before her death but hadn't. Her visitation felt more real than real and reassured me greatly. I felt encouraged to see her well and surrounded by loved ones. Unbeknownst to me at the time, the dream heralded my mother's re-entrance into my life through my dreams.

Later that month, I had another dream in which I heard my mother's voice speak out of soft darkness saying, "I'm so sorry. If I'd known what you were, I would have raised you differently. I didn't realize." Her words haunted me for some time. Her voice communicated a yearning, like a lament, whose meaning I could intuit but not articulate.

In the first dream, I had asked her for forgiveness. Now she sought mine. What she'd said to me made me wonder about the ways in which I did not know her or myself. In the dream, I sensed her deep, frustrated desire to be an artist and writer, her wish to live in a beautiful place and to travel to Europe — longings she never realized, except vicariously through me.

Upon waking, I recalled the sweet motifs she drew for a mural in the children's ward at the hospital in San Francisco, where she had worked as a nurse for a few years before meeting my father and their marrying six months later. In a photo taken at her graduation from nursing school, she wore her nursing cap with such pride, yet after her second year of marriage, when she became pregnant with my eldest brother, Steve, she took it off, never to wear it again. Following Steve's birth, the family moved to Okinawa where my father was serving as a dentist in the US Air Force during the Korean War, paying back Uncle Sam for funding his dental school training. At the time, the excitement of being a new mother and living in exotic surroundings far from the depression-era of her childhood must have been intoxicating.

Those years in Okinawa forever remained the days of martinis-and-magnolias in my parents' memories. The high-life ended when Dad refused to renew his tour of duty because he wasn't going to have some "son of a bitch" with a higher rank telling him "what-was-what." After he left the service, my parents decided they wanted to live where the sun shone year-round, so they set their sights on Southern California, instead of Northern California, where they had first met.

By the time they moved to the city of Orange, my mother

was nearly nine months pregnant with me. Determined to settle before my birth, my parents decided to buy what was meant to be a temporary home in a new suburban tract. Mom described the move in the summer heat of 100 degrees Fahrenheit as "Hell". They ended up living in that house on Garfield Street for nearly forty-years.

Returning to London after my mother's death, I found my doctoral studies in Psychology of Religion, once so absorbing, dry and lifeless. I longed to work in a more direct and meaningful way with others, so I left my post as a college Research Associate to train as a psychotherapist instead.

Seeking to come to terms with my mother's death and to share what I had learned from being with her, I also volunteered in a London hospice, sitting alongside the terminally ill during their last days and hours so that they would not die alone. Around this time, I had a dream that gave me a new perspective on my mother and life:

> *My mother and I float together in the sky, a few hundred feet apart. A silver cord about an inch thick connects us. I realize that if I look through it, I will see her better. Then it occurs to me that without it, I will see her even more clearly. Now lucid, I throw the cord aside. In that moment, the essence of my mother's being hits me full force. For the first time, I see her truly as an individual and feel even more grateful for her.*

When I shared this lucid dream with some colleagues on the psychotherapy training, one of the women, who was well-versed in esoteric teachings, exclaimed, "You saw the silver cord?! You don't know how lucky you are!" Apparently, this cord, usually invisible, connects us to the astral or spiritual realm. What seemed more important to me, however, was that the moment the cord fell away, I received this moving impression of my mother as a real person. Her artistic gifts, her sensitivity to beauty, her gentleness, and the sweetness of her soul, struck me powerfully.

The "Silver Cord" dream left me feeling both touched and torn, for I saw something in her that I had not yet fully recognized in myself. Together, these dreams made me wonder whether my mother, too, might understand me differently since her passing. Could she now recognize our shared longings? Could she sense how her resentment at "having" to stay in the marriage reached me in the womb?

When she was still alive, I once asked her if something about her pregnancy with me had been difficult even though the occasion of having a girl had been greeted with happiness. To my surprise, for the first and only time, she then told me how she had planned to leave Dad when my brothers were little, but finding out she was pregnant left her feeling she could not go through with a divorce. She added that although she loved me, from the moment the nurses placed me on her breast, she felt that she would never truly understand me. Years later, it came to me that it was herself she hadn't been able fully to understand and express. For so many of us, it would seem, this learning continues throughout our lives and into the next.

My Mother's Gifts

The three dreams that follow took place five years after my mother's death. By this time, I had begun the first year of my studies in psychotherapy, along with my second and final year of training in yoga. I told myself I was developing body, mind, and Spirit, but the trainings also distracted me from my personal sadness on account of difficulties in my first marriage.

My mother now began to appear more often in my dreams. These dreams followed a pattern in which I would first spend time in prayer, repeating a sacred name or singing a song of praise from the Christian tradition in which I was raised. In this first dream, "Soul Space", the setting of a newly renovated room suggests that an ongoing process of inner transformation had been taking place.

I barely recognize my newly renovated bedroom from childhood. Indian tapestries of gold, blue and red now line the walls. To my surprise, a large round white bed with a multi-tiered fountain in its center fills the room. On the top of the fountain, stands a silver statue of Shiva in his ring of fire. The entire structure somehow tracks the movement of the sun and the moon.

On the dresser, four more silver sculptures of gods and goddesses are displayed. I admire them and then go out into a central passageway that has four doors opening onto it. Against the far wall stands an altar down which water streams and alongside plants grow. A god made of silver is mounted at the top.

Then I sense a presence and turning around, I'm stunned to see my mother — aglow with beauty and confidence. She stands opposite me and smiles. As I cry out, "I love you", she reaches out to caress me.

Realizing she has appeared to me in a dream from beyond the grave, I embrace her, saying, "So it's true, we really will be able to spend time with each other again!?" She nods affirmatively and smiles. She seems very wise and looks at me reassuringly as if to say, "When it's time, there's nothing to fear." Abruptly, I find myself entering a boutique wanting to buy a coat of many colors. There, the dream ends.

With hindsight, I can see how the changing dreamscape portrayed my inner world at the time. The round bed and square room symbolized the elusive squaring of the circle, an image of integration between the ego and deeper self. Alchemically, the elements of fire and water, together with the presence of the sun and the moon, pointed to a powerful inner alignment. The qualities of the Divine, given form in statues of various gods and goddesses, infused me with awe and wonder, putting me in touch with a more soulful way of being.

In the dream, the central passageway with four doors marked a movement towards my inmost self, the Holy of Holies where the altar stands, one that holds a larger sense of the sacred Self.

Then, my mother appeared, reassuring me that we shall

have time together not only in the life to come but also, it would seem, in my dreams! Her subtlety and radiance reminded me of my desire for a more creative and spiritual life, hence my sudden longing for a coat of many colors. For me, this alluded to the biblical story of Joseph's coat of many colors, his talent for dreaming and his love for God. My mother's presence brought this soul longing to my consciousness.

In a dream a few months later, "The Dress", she helps me to choose a garment signifying the soul's inner splendor:

My mother and I have gone shopping for a new dress for me. I'm aware that she has died five years before and that she looks unusually well and youthful in the dream.

We enter a white, square-shaped shopping center with three levels: two above the ground and one below, with an open atrium in the center that connects all the levels, allowing the sun to stream in through a glass dome.

After some searching, we find the dress in the far back corner of the last shop, high on a rack. I ask the clerk for a hook to get it down. This off-the-shoulder dress has a bodice made of a fabric of white clouds set against a deep blue sky, tinged with purple and green. A royal blue sash hugs the waist and a fine blue ribbon the neck. The dress has a wide, white skirt made of large panels of linen or cotton.

Although I would like to put the dress on, I recall having read somewhere that new dresses can symbolize death, and this concerns me. I fear that if I put on the dress, death may come for me. It crosses my mind that it is hardly fair for me to die when I've only just learned so much about myself and life. Then I wake up!

Reflecting on this dream now, I see the setting as mirroring the previous dream but on a larger scale. Here the tiers of the fountain are echoed in three levels of the shopping center, which I understand as the three realms of Matter, Imagination, and Spirit. All coalesce in the atrium, vibrant with Spirit. I intuit that the architecture of the dream corresponded to a growing capacity within me to re-engage with life.

The colors of blue and white in the dress repeat the blue and white tones of the house where I had received the first visitation of my mother in the weeks after her death. For me, the colors blue and white impart a sense of a transcendent clarity and purity. Additional colors had begun to appear: purples, greens, reds, all colors imbued with the powerful vitality of life.

In the dream, I so want to wear this dress, yet the prospect of doing so frightens me. I remain caught up in the emotions of my childhood, afraid to be seen or to stand out lest I attract attention that could result in unwanted repercussions.

Upon waking from the dream, I understood what needed to die was this old way of being, one in which I still feared the life changes that wearing the dress would require of me.

That same night, I had another dream, "My Mother's Death":

My mother is resting in the bed I used in my mid-twenties. Mindful that she is going to die, I am cleaning the room in preparation for her death.

Dust covers the untidy room. I vacuum, sweep from under the bed, and wipe down the room, ending with changing the bedsheets to clean white cotton.

I feel great compassion for my mother, for all she has

suffered and for how hard she has tried to care for the family. She has done her utmost for me and my brothers as well as my father. In return, this is what I can do for her now.

Suddenly, a beautiful new piece of inlaid wooden furniture in the room captures my attention. The cabinet's curving sides house eight drawers of various sizes, some opened, some closed. When did my mother get this wonderful piece? I know that she wishes to pass it on to me.

The mysterious beauty of the eight-drawered cabinet later reminded me of Salvador Dali's artworks on the theme of "The Anthropomorphic Cabinet", in which he portrays the human body as housing a cabinet of drawers, each one showing where the body holds its unconscious contents. The dream indicated to me that much of my emotional and mental energy, previously held back by conditioned patterns, was being released through my training and therapy. The cabinet's beauteous presence spoke of spiritual potentialities and ascending states of awareness, which I connected with the chakra system of the East and their associated subtle energies

Pointedly, in this dream, my mother's deathbed was the same bed that I had bought for myself in my early twenties. It was time to let go of my outworn way of seeing my mother so that I could begin to take possession of the creative "mothering" aspect of my own being.

Importantly, at this time in my life, my then husband and I learned that as a couple we were going to face problems having children together. As a first step, I would start a course of IVF treatments. The night before I began the medication, I had the dream next described, one that involved my mother, and would radically change my understanding of the many ways people give birth to new life in the world.

The Dark Womb of Creation

In the months prior to this next dream, my mother's presence in my dreamlife coincided with my own growing capacity for lucid dreaming. The dream presented here suggests a direct connection between the two rather than mere coincidence. By this time, my experience of lucid dreaming had initiated me into the importance of surrender to the Divine through cultivating stillness and an open heart at the onset of lucidity.

I was discovering that when I took a stance of heartfelt surrender to the Divine, the dreamscape gave way to an infinite, formless expanse of luminous darkness, which I describe as "Black Light". Simultaneously, my dreambody would transform into a subtle body seemingly made of this same dark brilliance. Through sacred surrender, as my projections were withdrawn from this formless space, its "emptiness" filled with numinosity: a magnetic sense of Presence, Intelligence, and Unitive Oneness, an epiphany of the "light of awareness" or "the light in darkness".

I found that with ever-deepening surrender, yet more profound lucid states arose. However, at the time of this dream, the encounter with the Black Light was still relatively new to me, and I often felt frightened of it. In the dream that follows, the reference to my mother helped me to trust what then followed as the resplendent blackness revealed its nature more fully to me. [1]

For clarity, I have described this dream in three parts, each followed by a short commentary:

> As the dream begins, I am walking down an empty London Street at dawn. To my left I notice a wooden door slightly ajar, and I enter.
>
> The door opens into a small, softly lit shop. A handsome man, slightly older than me, is dozing behind the counter and wakes up as I enter. It surprises me to see that a bed takes up most of the shop. A thick, rumpled, golden cover drapes over the bed, its velvet folds catching the light and shadows in a mesmerizing way. The man, a jeweler, tells me he's made a "bauble" for my mother. He says this as though she is alive, although in the dream I know that she had died some years before.
>
> As he holds the jewelry up to the light, I see this "bauble" is, in fact, a necklace made of large solid gold squares hung around a gold chain. He asks, "Isn't her name Margid or Majid?" "Margaret," I reply. "Oh yes, that's it," he responds. Starting to become lucid, I recognize this word "Majid", for I had used it during a Sufi meditation in my waking life. It is Arabic for "majesty", one of the qualities Sufis associate with the Divine. It is evident to me that the word "majesty" also refers to my mother.
>
> Knowing that I don't have enough money to buy this priceless necklace, I ask if my mother has paid the deposit. "She has already paid the full price," he tells me, and smiles.

This dream began with a heightened sense of the incongruities and paradoxes that I have found often proceed full lucidity. For example, when the jeweller first mentions my mother, I wonder why the man spoke of her as if she were alive.

On reflection, I can see that the necklace symbolizes my spiritual inheritance, a gift beyond any price and conveyed through my mother's love, an expression of the Spirit's long-suffering, mothering love for Creation. The dream continues:

After giving me the necklace, the man moves to the bed, where I notice a clock that reads 6:30 in the morning. As I realize that it really is 6.30 a.m., my dream state now becomes fully lucid. Jubilant, I bow my head and wait breathlessly. In an instant, the dreamscape falls away and my dreambody disappears. My soul is carried on a powerful current of wind across the bright darkness, this time at an incredible speed, faster and further than ever before. For a moment, I panic, until I hear the Holy name of Gabriel and begin to repeat it. I become calm, conscious of two invisible presences that take me through a galaxy of stars.

The stars are sentient Beings, intelligent, radiant, and full of life, breathtakingly beautiful, each one unique. They encircle an immense, luminous, black center that they worship and reflect as they slowly, almost imperceptibly, orbit around. The two unseen presences lead me to the very center of this shining emptiness. There they "leave" me — or my very tiny point of consciousness — hovering in a space that feels firm and soft at the same time. From this central point, the sparkling blackness radiates around me as if I were on the top of the highest mountain in the world surrounded by the silent spaciousness of the night sky. I experience both exultation and apprehension.

This second part of the dream began in silence, no words, or thoughts, only quiet anticipation. As the dreamscape gave way to formlessness, the energy within the limitless field of glowing darkness nearly overwhelmed me even though unseen Beings accompanied me. Hearing Gabriel's name voiced on the apparent "void" reminded me that calling on a sacred name would help me to find my breath and calm my mind.

Knowing that my mother had made this experience possible, I was more able to entrust myself to whatever occurred. When I stopped resisting the flow of energy that carried me and accepted the two invisible presences without needing to know more about them, then the great expanse of starlike Beings materialized.

And yet, within the vast immensity of Black Light in which my soul was placed, fearful thoughts initially kept me from surrendering fully to the Holy Presence:

Suspended in the void, I feel bereft, lost, as if there is no way to know what this mystery is or who I am. But recalling the velvety darkness of previous dreams, I wait for a long time, repeating the Holy name until I sense that this radiant blackness supports and sustains me — giving me life. So how could it harm me? I feel one with this mysterious dark light and at the same time found, known and loved. As the dazzling darkness moves through me, I know that I, too can love as I am loved.

Feeling moved to dance, I raise my right arm up into Natarajasana — the Lord Shiva's Dance pose in yoga, noticing that my arm has now become a beam of light. I am filled with joy, alive with the inner light of this shimmering mystery and the multitude of worshipping stars.

As if on cue, the two unseen presences lift me up and guide me back through the stars to my earthly body asleep in my bed. It is seven o'clock as I awaken, feeling rested and safe, and sure all will be well.

This dream I called "The Ka'ba", after the Holiest site of Islam, which houses a venerated, black stone.

The very next day my hopes of having a child through IVF were shattered when I had a severe allergic reaction to the initial medication. This would make it impossible to continue with the treatments. During the time of illness and grief that followed, this dream comforted me. It felt as if my mother had known what would happen and had "paid in advance", to ensure that I had the precious energy needed to retrieve my soul and rekindle my love for life. This dream, I am sure, was sent as a touchstone, a reminder that I, indeed all of humanity, exist in love, no matter our personal sadness or suffering.

Back Home Again

In the years following the dream "The Dark Womb of Creation", my involvement in the outer world expanded, together with my capacity for lucid dreaming. In my final year of training as a psychotherapist, I became the manager of a charitable counselling center, where I had been volunteering as counsellor for a year. The following year, I was appointed director.

Working in a therapeutic context made me more conscious of how the family dynamics of my childhood shaped my responses to others, an inner process also mirrored in my dreams at this time, particularly the one described in this chapter. Here, I need to give some background information about my family to set the context for the dream's imagery.

Not long after my birth, my father decided to buy a camper mounted on a 1962 Ford pickup truck for family vacations in the great outdoors of the American Southwest. My mother had grown tired of cooking over an open fire and sleeping in tents that leaked or blew down in rainstorms. Dad thought he could convince her to come on camping trips if she had a real stove, a comfortable bed, and shelter from storms.

I was only three-years old when my parents bought the camper, but I can still recall going to the sales lot with them and finding the camper we would one day affectionately call "Old Lurch". We called her this because as she aged, she listed to the side, weighed down by all my dad's tools and travelling gear. The day my parents bought Old Lurch, her wood cabinets glowed warmly, and her blue curtains shone royally.

Over the years, Lurch would both transport our family and tow what Mom called my dad's "toys", over some 200,000 miles. In the late 1960s, Dad's main hobby was his 1949 army jeep, known as Willy. Lurch hauled Willy to dropping off points in the canyon lands of Utah and the back roads of the Mojave Desert. In the early seventies, Dad and my brothers welded metal tubes together in our garage to build a "dune buggy", complete with a one-hundred-and-forty horse-power Corvair engine. World War II parachute straps were made into seatbelts, and smooth, oversized tires were mounted on the back for driving on the sand dunes of Southern California.

To tow the dune buggy, Dad gave Old Lurch a V-8 engine that could pull the two-ton load up steep, winding roads. He would say, "She doesn't look like beans on the outside, but boy she can pull a load." Old Lurch towed the dune buggy to places like Dumont Dunes and the Borrego Badlands. In the 1970s, when gas prices made dune buggy trips too expensive, Dad used Old Lurch to take fishing equipment and the family up to the Sierra Nevada Mountains.

Camping trips were my father's consolation for the hours he spent cooped up in his family dental practice a few miles from our home on Garfield Street. When Dad was a teenager, he decided to become a dentist so he could escape the drudgery and financial insecurity of working on the family farm in Ogden, Utah. As it turned out, he found out that dentistry could be drudgery too. To top it off, the high overhead costs of running the business, coupled with the heavy tax burden, siphoned off his profits, leaving Mom crying that she couldn't afford to feed and dress a family of five on what my dad brought home. Frustrated by the fine work he did for hours on end, his dwindling profits, and the responsibility of being the "sole provider", Dad paced his office like a caged bear, muttering under his breath, "Goddamn it to hell and back, what kind of shit life is this anyway?"

For years, Mom worked at Dad's dental clinic as a receptionist. My brothers worked there too, Carey as Dad's assistant and Steve in the lab learning to make porcelain and precious metal crowns. From my early teens, I trained up as a part-time chairside assistant and worked in the office until my mid-twenties, before leaving for Europe.

Watching Dad, I never understood how he maneuvered his massive hands around his patients' mouths. Dad stood six feet four inches tall and weighed around two hundred pounds. He constantly had back pain from hunching over his patients and in his later years was plagued by tinnitus in his right ear that sounded like his own high-pitched drill. He also may well have had mercury poisoning from the amalgam fillings he did by the thousands — possibly contributing to his dramatic mood swings, no doubt fueled by the Molotov cocktail of money worries, tranquilizers, and whiskey churning in his gut.

Those first years after my parents moved to Garfield Street were full of promise. I didn't realize it until decades later, but my mother, at thirty-eight, and Dad, at thirty-five, had started over again in mid-life with a move to the town of Orange in Orange County, then famous for its many orange groves and the train depot near our house that shipped fruit back East until the early 1970s. Dad had high hopes of a booming practice and doing well financially. In the waiting room of his dental office, he set up an aquarium filled with angelfish and a small treasure chest that opened and shut, in response to air bubbles from the filter. The chest, full of imitation jewels and gold, seemed a promise of good things to come.

In anticipation of their future success, Mom and Dad hired a decorator to make their home a place for entertaining. They covered the top half of the dining room wall with a mirror that had real gold leaf etching on it and looked vaguely like a topographical map. They bought a mahogany dining table with an extension for dinner parties and hung ivory colored, floor-to-ceiling curtains with peacock trim in both the dining and living rooms. The fabric matched the turquoise-blue silk chairs and the weave of gold, blue, and green in the couch, complementing the marble top coffee table. Even as a toddler, I could feel the hope in the air.

Over the years, this hope dimmed along with the fading furniture, an outward expression of the distress that we all felt inwardly. First Mom's ivory curtains got stained dishwater-brown during a fire that raged nearby in the dry hills, sending down a blizzard of ash over our neighborhood. Then the dining and coffee tables began to show water stains and got chipped in the corners where my brothers and I ran into them when we chased each other around the house. (Those hard corners gave us gashes in our foreheads and knees that Dad patched up with stitches and butterfly bandages.) With time, the silk turquoise-blue chairs and fancy couch got worn and dirty. Even Old Lurch's wooden cabinets dulled and chipped, her curtains torn and faded. Only the gold leaf etching on the mirror in the dining room remained pristine.

I think my mother first began to give up hope when Dad started to dig out the foundation for the atomic bomb shelter that he and my brothers built. My mom, brothers, and I had argued for a pool, but Dad, nervous about fallout from the Cuban Missile crisis, thought a bomb shelter made more sense. Mom ruefully joked that the bomb shelter — twelve feet deep and ten feet wide — would serve as the family tomb. In a way, her dire prophecy held some truth — a part of each of us got buried there amidst the dirt, wood, steel, and cement that went into making it.

Dad maintained that he had my brothers help him build the bomb shelter so they could learn some basic building skills and, in the process, come to realize that they had better study hard in school so they could get comfortable office jobs. After Dad's early years of working on his family's farm, he was determined to have his sons prepare for white-collar professions. His thinking went, "I'll show them what a bitch it is to work with your hands." My brothers always maintained that they could have learned that lesson just as well by building a swimming pool. Steve was twelve at the time, Carey ten, and I was three. All of us dreamed of whiling away the hot summers splashing in a pool. Instead, we got the bomb shelter.

Dad got building plans for the shelter from the Civil Defense office. Chilling memories of Nikita Khrushchev taking off his shoe and slamming it down on the podium during an anti-US speech at the United Nations hammered away in my dad's mind, echoing throughout the building of the bomb shelter. The shelter with its deep *L*-shaped entrance may have provided a layer of protection between us and the fallout from an A-bomb, but it couldn't have saved us from re-entering a devastated world after a nuclear attack.

As I got older, I could see that building the bomb shelter had been as pointless as the duck-and-cover drills that schools required to prepare students for a nuclear attack. On the warning signal of a wailing siren, the whole class had to huddle under our desks and cover our heads with our hands. As Dad himself later said of such drills, in reality, "They weren't worth a hill of beans."

Dad rigged the bomb shelter with lights, a blue dial-phone, a desk, and a bunk bed. None of us ever asked why there weren't enough beds for all of us! My brother Steve added a punching bag that reverberated through the neighborhood under his rapid-fire punches. Even on hot summer days, the bomb shelter was cool, so Dad used it to store extra cans of oil for the cars, Old Lurch, Willy, and later, for his dune buggy. I don't recall that we ever stored food or water supplies down there. Steve used the place as a make-out pad. My girlfriends and I climbed up and down the bars of the precipitous entranceway like monkeys. Carey simply avoided going into the bomb shelter once it was finished.

Building the bomb shelter was hell for my brothers. Dad, Steve, and Carey hauled a mountain of excavated soil to an empty lot where a shopping mall was later built. Just when they were ready to pour cement over the concrete blocks that they had laid on the floor and mounted on the sides between steel support rods, the rains came. For months the hole had to be bailed out. Heavy with rainwater, the sides caved in, and so they had to haul out more dirt and reset the steel rods.

It took over a year to complete the bomb shelter. I don't think my dad ever counted the costs, but my brothers certainly did. Carey, who became a doctor, bought a house with an enormous blue pool in the backyard. When Dad came to visit his family, he teased, "I finally got my pool Dad." Dad smiled knowingly, no doubt convinced that the bomb shelter's object lesson had propelled Carey into the medical profession. Yet, digging out the shelter's foundation and building up its walls nearly broke my brothers. If ever one of them complained, Dad showed no mercy, saying, "What are you, a wimp? You big sissy!"

One afternoon when Dad and my brothers were working out back, I heard Dad shouting and saw Dad lift Steve by his shirt and hurl him against the garden wall. Steve slammed into it and slid down without a sound.

I always felt bad about this traumatic memory because it seemed I did nothing to make Dad stop. But many years later, my mother told me that when I saw what happened, I started crying hysterically. That night, for first time ever, I had a nightmare. When Dad saw how I reacted, he stopped hitting Steve.

It didn't occur to me then to ask Mom why she couldn't stop my father or why she didn't take more concrete steps to protect her children. She often told me she was sure that I was born to protect my brothers because whenever Dad shouted at them, I'd start bawling, and he couldn't stand that, so he'd stop his yelling. I remember wishing she wouldn't say that about me. In my forties, I understood that I had been the real bomb shelter.

To get some relief from the tensions of work, Dad would

load up the camper and take us all to explore places in the Southwestern United States, like the Grand Canyon, Monument Valley, Route Sixty-Six, Joshua Tree, and Lone Pine in the Eastern Sierras, occasionally venturing as far afield as Yellowstone National Park in Wyoming and the Big Sky country of Montana. The excursions were well-intended but Dad's unpredictable anger, matched by my mother's seething resentment, followed us out on the road, causing us children to be fearful and vigilant. As Steve later remarked, "Those trips were always beautiful adventures, but I wouldn't describe them as fun."

Almost every month, Old Lurch steadfastly carried our family from one natural wonder to another. But when I turned nine, Mom declared that she wouldn't be going camping anymore, and by this time my brothers were teenagers and too "cool" to go fishing with Dad and me, so he and I would set out alone.

Mom once explained to me that she thought it was fine for me to go with Dad because he was less tense about raising a girl. As he saw it, you didn't have to worry about teaching a girl how to be a man (though you could make a good tomboy out of her). And you didn't hit little girls. With a girl, you could go a bit easier, though his idea of "easy" often resulted in me crying quietly to myself on stamina-building backpacking trips. That was how Mom rationalized sending me out into the wilds with my father on our own. At the same time, I can say now that it wasn't right for me to be taking her place, most probably, so that she could "get a break" from Dad. Looking back, however, I wouldn't wish to have forgone those trips now, for they were as beautiful as they were hard.

It is no accident that the following lucid dream, "Night Sky" begins with me riding in Old Lurch to an unknown destination:

> *As the sun sets, I watch it from the top bunk of our family's camper, where I am resting. The sun's light has a striking intensity that reminds me of the Spirit. I'd like to get out of the camper and stand directly in the light, but I am so very tired that I give in to the weariness.*
>
> *Finally, as night falls, it occurs to me that I can open the sky light over the camper's upper bunk to see the sky more clearly. The stars shine like diamonds and fill me with joy. I suddenly feel moved to seek out my father to thank him not only for giving me access to Nature's wonders but also for giving me life and caring for me until I could care for myself.*
>
> *In a flash, I find myself seated with my family at the dining table in the house where I grew up, but everything looks new. My parents are surprisingly calm and contented. I see them as individuals yet at one with the mystery of their union, two souls who brought the gift of life to their three children. For once, we all sit round a table ready to share a meal, uncharacteristically relaxed and at ease. Then I wake up.*

With the passage of time, I have come to see the opening of the skylight in the upper bunk as representing the opening of my mind to a more kind-hearted view of my parents, one in which I was being given the chance to see my parents and childhood with the "eye of the heart". This helped me to understand how the difficulties of the past led to my spiritual awakening in dreams.

On a subtle level, the skylight can be likened to the crown chakra of the Hindu tradition, which aligns us with the Spirit's will. As I worked therapeutically on my personal psychology and dreams, my lucid dreams, like this one, became increasingly luminescent, reflecting a growing understanding of the power of the Holy Spirit to turn sorrow into joy and resentment into forgiveness.

When my parents put the house on Garfield Street up for sale, the saleswoman sighed wearily the moment she saw the bomb shelter. But surprisingly, the shelter didn't slow the sale. A family with a twelve-year old boy bought our house, and he made the bomb shelter his own clubhouse, cool even on hot days. The next family to move there turned the bomb shelter into a wine cellar. However, the family after that had the bomb shelter removed entirely. Neighbors complained that for weeks the sound of drills on concrete reverberated through Garfield Street.

When Dad retired, he sold his practice. Everything in the dental office went to the new owners, even the 1970s mood lamp that dripped oil in droplets on strings around a statue of a naked woman standing amidst plastic ferns. To my surprise, when I was helping my brothers clean out Dad's garage after his death, I came across the dust-covered aquarium. The treasure chest had disappeared, seemingly along with my parents' hopes for a golden future. I'm not sure if they ever knew, as in the relaxed family meal of my dream, that the real "treasure" was the family itself, all along. I sometimes wonder if my mother, recognizing this truth on the other side, has sought to make amends through my dreams.

Mirroring Soul

After many further lucid dreams, I noticed that a threshold, whether a skylight, window, door, or a mirror, as in the dream that follows, often marks the onset of lucidity. Such dream imagery signifies a potential crossing or "limen" to a deeper realm of experience.

I can clearly recall the first time that a mirror became a "door" to a new dimension, namely the Black Light of the lucid void. Once I had passed through the mirror into an endless shining darkness, a portal appeared on the void in the form of a dodecahedron made entirely of golden light.

Such portals often lead to places where memories from my past are re-visited with the eyes of Love. Once again, my mother's presence in the initial scene enables me to trust the unusual events that follow in the dream of "Entering the Mirror":

> *I rest in a four-poster bed, one that I bought in my late teens. My mother rests peacefully beside me and next to her lies a college boyfriend of mine who, when I knew him, was a gifted artist. Noticing a new blue vase and yellow glass rose on the dresser, I go to look at them. The beauty of the three-part antique style mirror over the dresser and the still light it reflects catches my attention.*
>
> *When I see my own reflection in the glass, I become lucid and bow my head in surrender. Immediately, my soul is*

pulled through the mirror and carried across the Black Light. Brightly colored, multi-dimensional geometric shapes fill the gleaming emptiness. Passing through an immense dodecahedron of golden light, I find myself in a place much like the Baptist church I attended in childhood.

A handful of women, exuding strength and independence, come out to greet me as if they already know me, stroking my face, hands, and arms. Their touch feels like the breath of the Holy Spirit, and I think of a line from a poem I once wrote: "The Spirit puts on your hands like gloves." New words come to me: "Touch skin."

As the women touch me, I sense they also receive something from me in a wordless, tactile exchange. We have all come to this place to learn of God. Teresa of Avila's poetry springs to mind: "Teach me, God, all you know." Abruptly, I tumble out of the mirror, back into the original dream.

Although my mother disappears once I pass through the mirror, her presence on the Black Light is symbolized by the place that emerged out of the seeming void. I feel this to be so because when my brothers and I were children, Mom faithfully took us to the local Baptist church right through until our teens. As children, we all found a sense of peace and containment there that we didn't feel at home.

The dream evoked memories of my mother singing in the choir at the church, where she also taught Sunday school. In church, next to me, her chin tilted upwards, her throat extended, she would sing joyfully, hitting the high notes far beyond my reach. Neither of us knew then that the refrains of hymns

I learned there would help me decades later to sustain dream lucidity, like "Holy, Holy, Holy, Lord God of Power and Might Heaven and Earth are full of your glory. Blessed is he who comes in the name of the Lord" and "Amazing Grace".

Dad only went to church for weddings. Mom said my father had attended Sunday services regularly in the months after my birth. He told the Pastor that he'd attend for a year, but after that, if he wasn't convinced, he'd stop going, in which case the Reverend wasn't to bother him anymore. Dad wasn't the contemplative type. He would say, "I can look at a nice view for ten minutes or so, then I need to be up doing something."

Even so, during our trips to the seaside, deserts, and mountains of California, he introduced me to Nature's sanctuary. I fondly recall sitting with my father on a massive granite boulder by a pristine lake in the Eastern Sierra Nevada Mountains of California. Resting there before our final ascent to the top of Mt. Whitney, which stands at over 14,000 feet, and warming ourselves in the sun, we shared a snack of high-energy raisins and nuts as we admired the jutting peaks surrounding us.

On arduous backpacking trips with my father, when, suffering from exhaustion, I found that by singing the songs and hymns from church and setting my steps to the rhythm, I could put myself in a kind of trance and find the energy needed to continue. The same sacred songs would similarly feature in the lucid dreams that later tested my soul stamina. One of these songs comes to mind now, as I recall my mother sitting on a chair in front of us six-year-olds in Sunday school. Her blonde hair framing her face and her vintage-style skirt spread around her, she led us in singing, "Little children, little children, who love their Redeemer, are the jewels, precious jewels, his loved and his own. Like the bright stars of morning, his bright crown adoring, they shall shine in his beauty, his loved and his own."

The women who came out of the church in my dream to greet me reminded me of the many fine women who, along with my mother, taught me Bible stories and verses. I recall reciting Psalm 23, "He leads me besides the still waters", to Mrs. Preston, our Sunday School teacher, and listening to Mrs. Yankowski telling us about the mysterious ways God speaks to human beings: out of a burning bush, a cloud, a whirlwind, or in silence and dreams. From such lessons, we children learned that biblical characters like Moses doubted and questioned God, while others, who knowingly disobeyed God's commandments, could still find forgiveness when they had a contrite heart. The essence of such teachings encouraged me in later years to trust the Holy Mystery of my lucid dreams and to share the learning from them, no matter my own human frailties.

Given these many memories of Sunday school, it makes sense that the women in the dream taught me through their healing touch. Yet, this communication between angelic Beings and myself was not one-sided. Rather, it seemed to be an exchange, as if by touching me they too were learning from my experience of waking life and dream lucidity. With hindsight, it occurs to me that the presence of my college boyfriend, an artist, likely represented the artistic leanings which my mother and I shared.

This lucid dream also delineated multiple levels of consciousness: I was cognizant of my waking life, my sleeping self, the initial form-based dream of my old bedroom, my own lucidity as I gazed at the mirror, beyond that, the formlessness of the Black Light, [2] and hence the visionary encounters that awaited me.

Most importantly for me, the caresses of the five women in my dream reminded me of my mother's hands. Through her loving touch, as the poem of my dream describes, she showed me how the Spirit puts on our hands like gloves to touch the world.

The Way to Blue

The three dreams I share here occurred over a four-month period filled with personal and professional challenges. In each dream, the color blue illumines truths about the nature of Soul and Spirit, helping me to transcend my personal difficulties. The guiding presence of my mother, in all these dreams, leads me more deeply into what the color blue can teach us.

The first dream "The Blue Mosque" is, as the name suggests, set at the Blue Mosque in Istanbul, Turkey.[3] In my waking life, when I first learned of the Blue Mosque in my mid-twenties, I determined to make a pilgrimage there. In my forties, I travelled to Turkey and was at last able to visit this hallowed site and before sharing the dream, I would like to describe what happened there.

Although I had visited synagogues and temples of many other faiths, this was my first mosque. By this time, the treasures of esoteric Islam had been introduced to me through the teachings of the twelfth-century Sufi Ibn 'Arabi. This spiritual teacher, writer and visionary taught that the union with the Divine can be experienced in dreams.

Before entering the mosque, I observed the Muslim tradition of ritually washing my hands and feet, as a symbol of purity, and donned a veil, as a sign of humility. In the main sanctuary, cascades of light poured through a multitude of blue and white domes that fanned out from the central dome, as if falling from a tiered fountain decorated with delicate vines and flowers.

In accordance with Islamic law prohibiting representations of animal and human forms, an infinite array of geometric, calligraphic, and floral patterns set against a background of white and lapis-lazuli blue covered the walls and domes, leaving my mind feeling naked and pure, as if bathed in light. The mosque's interior, like the architecture of a lucid dream resplendent with light and color, revealed the Divine's Majesty and Beauty. Profoundly moved by the Blue Mosque's inner sanctuary, I found myself in tears, washed through with Spirit.

My brief but intense dream of the Blue Mosque, which occurred many years later after my visit to it, contrasts starkly with what I had experienced in my waking life!

> *I am standing with my mother at the entranceway to the mosque's inner courtyard. My mother tells me that she needs to use the toilet. I suddenly decide we cannot enter the Blue Mosque, saying, "No, no we don't have the appropriate headscarves to enter". There the dream ends.*

Upon waking, I recognized a familiar pattern: when I begin to approach the Holy, the inner sanctum where the Spirit dwells in each of us, conventional concerns distract me. My fears in this dream caused me to pass up the opportunity to visit to the Blue Mosque. Perhaps, too, I sense my lack of inward preparation to encounter the Holy.

Contemplating this, I feel chagrin. I can now see how the constructs of my conditioned mind close the door to my soul's longings. Even though my mother and I did not go beyond the Blue Mosque's inner courtyard, the very sight of the Mosque evoked the spiritual dimension within me. This dream seems to pose a question voiced by the Apostle Paul: "Do you not know that you yourselves are God's temple, and the Spirit of God dwells in you?",[4] reminding me that God does not live in temples made by human hands but in the heart.[5]

The second dream, "On the Breath", coming a few weeks later, builds upon the learning from the first. Here the blue takes on an added depth and brilliance, reflecting the pure light of unbounded Being without reference to a form or object outside itself:

> *At the outset of the dream, I am arguing with my former husband over which of us is more alone in this world. I say, "I have left my country, my family; both my mother and dear aunt have died, and my father hardly knows me [with his dementia]." Then I see my mother, who shakes her head side to side as if to say, "You are not alone."*
>
> *With the realization that she is dead in waking life, I become lucid, and at once, my soul is carried a long way in radiant darkness. I repeat a sacred name until a dazzling azure blue space opens up around me. The infinite blue feels like it encompasses Creation. The blue overwhelms me, and I prostrate myself, crying out, "Forgive me, God, for every time I have forgotten your blue on the breath." I say this moved by gratitude for all the beauty and wonder I must have failed to appreciate fully before.*
>
> *Then I see what appear to be piercing white clouds on the*

horizon. Beyond them, the brilliant blackness returns, and I am carried back on the winds of this effervescent blackness until I wake up, recalling a line from a Sufi teacher: "The only sin is to forget God on the breath."

Whereas negative thoughts in the first dream kept me from entering the Blue Mosque, this time my mother's response to my ego-bound discontent enabled me to see the error of childish reproaches. Since she and the Spirit are always with me, how can I ever be truly alone?

Once I accepted her guiding presence and let go of my own resentments, the dream then conveyed the inner meaning of blue. The blue immersed me in the joy and beauty that abides at the core of life. I felt the reality of all-encompassing love and without judgement. The blue relieved the thirst within me to feel fully present to life itself. Against this backdrop, my personal concerns were transcended and seen from a new perspective.

At the time of this dream, I felt I was losing my innocence of heart. My immersion in the blue assured me of the soul's essential purity. The challenge for me would be to trust in, and live by, the soulful quality of that intense blue. However, my third dream, a month later, reminds me what a challenge that would be:

The dream opens with me standing in the entranceway to the family home on Garfield Street. My mother is preparing lunch in the kitchen. A man with whom I once had an extramarital affair (in actuality) is coming to see me. I wait for him by the front screen door, feeling both excited and fearful.

He arrives in a white van with two men. Looking uncharacteristically angry, he storms towards the door, stopping about thirty feet away. To everyone and no one, he shouts: "I could either kill her or kidnap her and take her with me!" One of his friends tells him to calm down and hand over what he's come to give me.

Then he throws a big red and white leather duffle bag towards the screen door. A little white puppy crawls out of the bag and pushes the screen open. When the puppy sees the van is driving off, it begins to bark incessantly. I let it out to chase after the van. The van stops and a door opens to let the dog in.

Then, one of the men gets out and walks back to me. Standing at the front door, he says, "Take this!", as he proudly holds up a blue, electric guitar. Initially, I am thrilled to be given the guitar, but then I wonder how I will explain to my family who the guitar has come from. Because of this, I tell the man I can't play music and turn away. Immediately, I understand that it was a mistake to refuse the gift. Then, I awake.

Sometime later, when reviewing this dream, which I named "The Blue Guitar", I recalled a poem titled, "The Man with the Blue Guitar" by Wallace Stevens, a poem evoking the mystery of creativity. I looked up the lines of the poem that had so touched me when I first read them in college. In this poem, a man who plays a blue guitar creates music that seems strange to others. When people tell him that he does not "play things as they are", he replies that things change when played upon the blue guitar. Then they say to him that he must go ahead and play his music:

> "A tune beyond us, yet ourselves,
> A tune upon the blue guitar
> Of things exactly as they are."

Overriding my heart's desire and refusing the gift of the blue guitar paralleled my inner resistance to Eros, the life-force at the heart of life, and mirrored my inability to acknowledge my instinctive creativity and spirituality. I can see now that the puppy, which embodied an innocent instinctiveness, a soulful quality, wished me to follow it, something which I felt I could not allow myself to do, neither in the dream nor in my life at the time. In the dream, failing to apprehend that there is more than one way to play the music of the soul, I refused the gift.

Thinking further on this dream, I can see that despite my mother's death, I still feared her disapproval because, unlike her, I had broken my marital vows. She once told me that she couldn't bear to hear about my own marital problems after trying to deal with her own and listening to the many troubles of family and friends. The message I had taken from her then was that she had stuck it out, so I should too. She had remained faithful so why couldn't I? However, in the dream, these fears of mine did not occur, as my mother remained a quiet presence in the kitchen, a place where she had often poured her heart out in song while preparing a meal or baking treats for the family. I like to think that now, from the life beyond, she views such life dramas with more compassion.

In contrast to my mother's calm, those words, "I could either kill her or kidnap her or take her with me!" had a prophetic tone. Upon waking, it struck me that my continued resistance to expressing my authentic and real self might result in my death. Even so, as my actions in the dream imply, I wasn't ready to make such changes. It would take another three years before I could bring myself to leave my marriage. Had I been able to accept a fuller expression of my soul, possibly I would have taken the step sooner. Nonetheless, because of the power and presence of the "blue" in my dreams, I felt encouraged to begin writing about my dreams and presenting them at dream conferences.[6] Sharing how the Spirit moves us in our dreams has proved to be a calling for me, the music of the soul, a "tune beyond ourselves and yet ourselves."

Part Two
Lessons in Light

The Holy of Holies

Earlier, I shared a dream in which, for the first time, a mirror served as a threshold to the lucid void. In that dream, my mother's presence reassured me that I could surrender to what was then new for me. Once through the mirror, I entered a building similar to the Baptist church that my mother had taken me to when I was growing up. In that dream, five angelic women came out to greet me, wordlessly communicating with me by stroking my face, arms and hair with their hands, their touch full of the Spirit's wisdom and love.

Nine months later, my mother once again figured in one of my dreams, which I call "The Fingerprint of God" because the lucid vision gave me the sense of being directly touched by Divine love. However, unlike the earlier dreams, in this instance, my mother entered the dream *after* I had become lucid rather than before. On this occasion, much to my surprise, she smiled at me from the *other side* of the mirror!

I have divided this dream into two halves: The first sets the scene for the revelatory lucid vision that follows on the "other side" of the mirror:

> *The dream begins in a shopping mall, and I am not happy about being there! It reminds me of the first enclosed mall built in Orange, California, where I was raised.*[7] *The shopping center brings up a familiar longing for something more natural and*

meaningful. I become lucid and say, "I know I'm dreaming, Lord, if you want to, come for me." As I do so, the dreamscape gives way to the Black Light, where a current of wind carries my soul very fast for a great distance. Repeating a sacred song helps me to keep focused.

The flow of energy carries me through stacked rows of golden hexagons that remind me of a honeycomb. Eventually, I am whisked into an unadorned tabernacle, with dark wood walls, a floor of lapis lazuli edged with mother of pearl, and a vaulted ceiling of sky-blue and white. The winds bring me to the front of the sanctuary, where two celestial Beings of light open a small arched door. With great joy I think, "The Holy of Holies! I am being permitted to enter in!"

I can see that behind the altar is a mirror, from which shines an intense, white light. I recall an Old Testament teaching warning that a searing light kills those who enter the tabernacle's inner sanctum unsanctified. For a moment, I feel afraid, conscious of my impurity. However, my joy outweighs my concern. I trust that this is where I should be since the Spirit has brought me here.

The reference to the "Holy of Holies" takes me back to how fascinated I was as a child by the Old Testament story of the Israelites "Tent of Meeting", a portable tabernacle that the Israelites made during their wanderings in the desert so that God could dwell among them. They constructed the Tabernacle from large curtains of woven blue, purple, and scarlet linen, embroidered in gold thread, which was draped over wooden frames and posts overlaid in gold.

The richly colored illustrations of the Tabernacle in the children's Bible book series that my mother bought for my brothers and me used to set my imagination alight with the wonder and mystery of how God inhabits the world. I remember feeling amazed that Moses climbed a high mountain to receive instructions for building the Tabernacle directly from God, who met with Moses in a black cloud on the mountaintop.

My mother used to sit with me on our living room couch while I read aloud tales of the Israelites' wanderings in the desert and their yearning for a place to call "The House of God". The colorful illustrations of the great Tabernacle in the desert thrilled me. Nothing I had ever seen in suburban Orange County compared.

The Tabernacle's layout especially attracted me. It was surrounded by an outer court, where people and priests gathered in the open air to burn sacrifices to God. The curtained Tabernacle had two parts, a "Holy Place" that only the priests could enter, and an Innermost Sanctuary, the "Holy of Holies", hidden behind a thick veil at the far end of the sanctuary.

This "Most Holy Place" beyond the veil, contained only one object, a wooden chest, covered in gold, "The Ark of the Covenant", which held mementos of God's love for the Israelites.[8] Atop the Ark, at either end, two cherubim made of gold faced one another, kneeling and shielding the treasured case with their outstretched wings. Between their wings, the Presence of God blazed as a cloud of fiery light. The Bible taught that the High Priest alone, who had been sanctified through sacrifices and prayer in the Holy Place could enter the Holy of Holies, [9] but only once a year. [10] Otherwise, he would be struck down dead by a blaze of piercing light.

In childhood, this teaching filled me with both fear and awe, a memory that carried into this lucid dream, making me even more frightened. Yet, my joy at the prospect of being taken into the Holy of Holies overcame my dread:

As the dream continues, I am brought closer to the mirror at great speed. In the mirror, I see my mother (who has died some years before) smiling radiantly at me against a backdrop of azure blue framing her blonde hair. I realize that I am about to pass through the mirror's surface and join my mother. Since I know my mother is dead, I wonder, "Does this mean I have died?" For once, I feel more curious than concerned. In a flash, my soul is taken through the mirror and released into the Black Light.

When I regain my equilibrium, an effulgent black cloud envelops me in love. I know this cloud from other dreams as the Divine Presence. I repeat, "Oh Holy One" and sing out hymns of praise with delight as the cloud whirls around and through me in a kind of dance. Suspended there, I am amazed to see a vast golden sphere, pulsing with swirls of golden light in a pattern akin to the whorls of a fingerprint. The thought comes: "The fingerprint of God! This is the true Holy of Holies."

A ruby red ball of light appears in its center and divides into two, emitting light that spills over its edges, embracing me, and piercing my heart. Part of me thinks, "This is what is meant by being in the sacred heart of Jesus!" There is humility, healing and hope in this realization. With this I am moved swiftly back through the red light back into the shopping mall, and at this point, I'm sure I have not died! Then I awake, my body alive with the pulsating light.

Given my fears about entering the Holy of Holies, it was a great comfort to see my dear mother's face looking out at me from the "other side" of the mirror. Her sweet smile, gentle expression, and clear blue eyes infused me with the trust needed to let the dream unfold, even though I feared that by "crossing over" to her, I may have died in waking life. In that instant, it felt as if we saw *into* one another, apprehending each other fully with one heart.

As I bring her countenance to mind now, I can recall one of my earliest memories of her bathing me as an infant in the kitchen sink, the afternoon light dancing on the water, her hair and in her loving, blue eyes. Little wonder, then, that my mother's radiant countenance in my lucid dream led me to the blessed heart of the Divine.

When comparing the structure of the Tabernacle with the unfolding dreamscape, it is evident to me that this dream's path follows the design of the Tabernacle. The dream begins in the outer world – the outer court – of everyday existence, depicted by a shopping mall. Lucidity marks a deeper shift into the inner world, where an attitude of self-surrender, a conscious "sacrifice" of the ego's demands is followed by the appearance of the sanctuary on the Black Light. Here, a mirror portrays the "veil", through which my soul is taken into the

Holy of Holies, filled with the Divine light.

Within the tabernacle of dreams, from beyond the "veil", my mother beckons me on to a Most Holy Place, overflowing with light and love. Immersed in this loving light, I feel touched by God. To enter this inner sanctum, one doesn't need to wear priestly garb, only to surrender the heart to Love, the way a mother surrenders her heart to her child or a lover to the beloved. "The Fingerprint of God" makes me appreciate that no matter where we find ourselves, we can find God, for all creation is the House of God and each one of us, a living light in which God dwells.

Trust in Light and Love

By the time of the lucid dream that follows, my mother had been dead for nine years. Yet, in my dreams, she not only lived but also seemed to be atoning for what she could not give me while alive, and so attending to unfinished business between us. In dream lucidity, she nurtured my soul nature far more than she was able to in life, bringing profound shifts in my understanding of light and love.

The dream "Ensoulment", shared here in four parts, helped me to understand more fully the transformation that my mother had undergone since dying and how her presence in my lucid dreams contributed to my spiritual growth. The beginning of the dream makes this change in my perception clear:

> *As I lie on my bed praying and drift off to sleep, my mother enters the room and lies down next to me. When I try to kiss her cheek, she has no physical solidity. With this, I realize she is dead and is now made of light. This insight strikes me as important, and I become lucid.*

While previously in dreams, I had tried to hold or caress my mother, it hadn't occurred to me that she no longer was made of flesh and blood, even though there was no strong sensation of physical touch. On this occasion, I perceived her for the first time as a *body* of light, a true Being of light. This realization both sparked lucidity and gave me the resilience needed for what followed:

> *Deeply joyful, my soul is carried on the Black Light a great distance. Polygons of light accompany me. The scene then changes into an immense, round hall made of ebony-colored wood and white-washed walls. Under a glass, octagonal dome, red, wooden chairs have been arranged in a circle for what I imagine will be a concert. The longing for music fills me and the thought comes, "Let there be musicians."*
>
> *Instead of this happening, the force that carries me drives me down through the floorboards at the hall's central point. I feel some confusion and concern as I smash through the wooden planks! Then, I remember that the usual physical laws don't apply in this reality, so all will be well. The unseen force seizes my soul and pulls me forwards in a steep descent harder and faster than ever before. I hear a voice that surrounds and protects me: "She is willing now to trust and be taken." It feels as if the Divine darkness itself takes pleasure in knowing that my yearning for God has overcome my fear.*

When revisiting this dream, it became apparent to me that its underlying structure shares many parallels with the dream "The Fingerprint of God" that preceded it a month before. Both follow a path that leads through a sacred sanctuary, across a threshold to a "Holy of Holies", where union with the Divine is known through loving light.

Each part of the dream's unfoldment has its own purpose.

The first begins even before sleep, through prayerful meditation. This stills the soul for sleep and dreams. The cultivation of concentration and soulful devotion continues through lucidity and onto the Black Light, where the ego's need to assert itself must be "sacrificed" to the Highest Will. In the second part, a Holy Place is revealed, taking the form of a sanctuary where truths about the soul's nature are made known. The unfolding dream takes the soul onwards through a threshold or "veil" to the Holiest of places, wherein dwells the Divine, the Source of all Creation.

In the round sanctuary of "Ensoulment", a longing for sacred music filled me, thus my request for musicians. Similarly, in the sanctuary of "The Fingerprint of God", I had felt moved to make the spontaneous request that candles appear to complete the setting. This time, however, my willful wish for musicians was not granted. Ensoulment was evidently the aim and purpose of lucidity.

Consequently, my soul was pulled powerfully on a downward path, breaking through the architecture of the dream into the infinite Black Light. The revelation that the physical laws of earthly life did not apply in dreams freed me from my fears. Yet without my mother having first come to me, I don't believe I could have allowed myself to be drawn down into the darkness.

The enigmatic voice that spoke tenderly out of the dream, remarking that I had learned to trust and to be taken, sounded neither male nor female, only affirming and true, like pure water. Was that the Spirit encouraging me? The flow of the dream drew my soul onwards too rapidly for me to speculate at the time.

Yet, the significance of that statement was not lost on me. Much therapeutic work revolves around learning to regain a sense of trust in our own intuition and in life itself, a trust that may have been violated, intentionally or not, by those we originally viewed with childlike faith, whether our parents, caregivers, or the wider world.

It seems to me now that my mother's mission in my lucid dreams was to help me re-establish trust in myself and in life. Through Lucid Surrender, her reassuring presence enabled me to rest in "being" and to "do nothing" so that in waking life I could find that still center, a wellspring of love that is the soul's nature and purpose:

> *As the dream continues, the steep descent does not bring the usual fear that I might be taken to Hell. Instead, I feel akin to how a droplet of water must feel as it tumbles into Niagara Falls, for this descent seems to be as endless as the universe.*
>
> *When the downward movement finally levels out, gentle winds impart an incredibly intense ecstatic pleasure. Yet a part of me wonders what I should do next. It feels hard to simply "be". The gleaming blackness holds me still, until at last, my heart gives way. Then the joyful emptiness and my soul become utterly permeable, each to the other ensouled in love.*

The paradox, shown to me in this dream is that instead of striving to be doing "something", it is by becoming "nothing" that I find myself in union with the Divine.

Being "bathed" in Spirit reminds me of my evening baths as a child. Closing the bathroom door, my mother would leave her worries outside the room, completely surrendering to innocent delight as she washed me tenderly. At such moments, she was at ease and fully present, unafraid. Bath time was sacred.

Afterwards, she would bring a warm towel to wrap me in, a tradition that would make her legendary amongst her grandchildren. My use of the word "bathed" to describe this lucid immersion in the Spirit resonates with childhood memories of cleansing innocence, spontaneous joy, and natural intimacy.

I am reminded, too, of the grown-up pleasure of sinking exhausted into a hot bath and feeling renewed with the waters of life. Sometimes doing nothing is everything!

> *Still dreaming, I am surprised to find myself "lifted" into a "normal" (non-lucid) dream in which my nephew and niece, the children of my eldest brother, are both getting married in a double wedding ceremony.*
>
> *I long to embrace my niece who wears a white, pearl-lined wedding dress. I tell her my happiness at being able to come from such a long way away to be at this wedding and how I regret that I did not attend her actual wedding.*
>
> *When I awake from this dream, the clock reads 10:30am.*

Upon waking, it takes me some time to lift my body from the bed. The lucid experience has felt like an intense purification, a cleansing and filling with overflowing energy.

This dream ended with a double-wedding, which I see as

mirroring the inner marriage of Spirit and Soul within me. I have always regretted missing my niece's wedding in waking life, for at the time, my grief at losing my mother not long before held me back. Imagine my joy in the dream at being given a second chance to be there for her wedding!

The journey of embodied life and of the Spirit are entwined, as this dream highlighted for me. Indeed, in the oneness of All, just as the flesh cleaves to bone, the Spirit cleaves to love and light.

The Body of Light

Through her presence in my dreams over the preceding months, my mother, like a wise Sophia figure, taught me to surrender to union with Divine light. Then, in a lucid dream, I received a 'letter from beyond the veil' in which she wrote that as she had gone before me, I had nothing to fear. She assured me that she would help to make "all in this life new". Her letter went on to say, "I will do what I could not do for you here [on Earth]. You only need to watch the future unfold."[11] Her words filled me with quiet confidence.

While still in the lucid dream, I recalled how a few years earlier, in another dream, my mother had also given me a letter. At the time, I had been thinking of separating from my then husband. In that first letter, she wrote that I must do what my heart told me and that she knew my heart's desire. She understood my need to take hold of the opportunity life had presented and added that I needn't base my actions on what I thought would have pleased others, herself included. Most affirming of all, she told me she loved me and was watching out for me. Her words gave me the will eventually to go ahead with this separation and helped me to make some difficult decisions in the years that followed.

Whereas her first letter encouraged me to act in my life as I saw fit, her second reminded me that no matter the circumstances of my outer life, through grace, I could know myself as the Beloved, at one with Spirit.

The next lucid dream involving my mother took place when pressures had been increasing at the charitable counselling center I was running. We faced closure unless we could raise an additional fifty-thousand pounds in the coming three months. As in the myth of "Psyche and Eros", in which Psyche labors under tasks so insurmountable they could only be completed with the help of Divine guidance and grace, I was feeling a burden of responsibility beyond my capability.

This night in question, before falling asleep, I had spent much time in prayer. In the lucid dream that followed, which I call "Body of Light", my mother revealed herself to me in an entirely new way.

The dream is presented here in two parts:

Initially, it seems that I am in the dining room of my family home where I grew up. The room has been newly renovated and sunlight streams in, which strikes me as strange since in waking life the room was usually shaded by a roof over the patio.

My sister-in-law, a minister, comes in looking worried. I say to her, "We are in a dream so there's no need to worry." I feel the love between us and our shared love of the Spirit. Then I remember that the dining room wall features a gold-lined mirror and turn to look at it. The room and my sister-in-law appear in the mirror, but my own reflection is not visible. At first this concerns me since I wonder if I have died, but then it occurs to me that from the spiritual perspective it must be a good thing, in that my ego defenses must have dissolved.

> *This insight brings lucidity and surrender as the dreamscape gives way to a vast field of glorious Black Light. A strong wind seizes my soul and carries me a great distance until the soles of my feet are set gently upon unseen ground. The moment this happens, it feels as though all the stones, plants, animals, and beings of this place rise through me, as if my soul has touched the fount of Life itself, surging upwards and taking complete hold of me. After that my memory goes blank for some time.*

By this time, many other lucid dreams had shown me that mirrors not only reveal aspects of our own nature but also can serve as portals to new dimensions, so I had been curious to see what the dining room mirror might reveal. However, this was one of the rare times I could not see my own reflection. The ensuing lucidity freed me to experience a profound awakening to the fullness and richness of all, infusing me with a fresh zest for living.

It seems fitting that this dream began in the dining room of my childhood home, a room that had once epitomized my parents' hopes for their future happiness.

When I was a child, the golden strands running across the mirror reminded me of a topographical map, but in this dream, it proved to be a "map" to the inner world and the challenge of overcoming my ego defenses so that I could know myself and the world in a new way. Hence the dining room's recent renovation in the dream.

Although my mother had not appeared directly in this part of the dream, her presence was symbolized by the gold of the dining room mirror, signifying her most treasured hopes for her family and herself. Through this part of the dream, I feel certain she knew that I would eventually be led to the riches of the inner life.

After this opening scene, the dreamscape abruptly shifted to me resting in my bed of my (then) home:

> *A male Being comes in and lies next to me, desirous of making love. His skin looks like obsidian, but he seems edgy and distracted, and my mind thinks, "An incubus". What bothers me most is that I am wanting to rest and contemplate the initial lucid dream. Also, given the Being's edginess, I am unsure whether he means me harm or good, so I sit up and start singing a hymn to Jesus, certain that the Being will disappear if the song doesn't suit him. I sing, "Jesus, name above all names, beautiful Savior, glorious Lord, Emmanuel, God is with us...." The Being slides away.*
>
> *Then I hear a woman taking up the tune in a sweet, high soprano. Instantly I am in a still, shining black space. I recognize this voice as my mother's. Out of the void appears a white sphere, inside of which a purple cube emits a large red, pulsating ball of light from its central point. The harmony and beauty of the form is breath-taking. My mother's voice comes from the innermost sphere of light. I understand this is how my mother's soul is being shown to me.*
>
> *Filled with love and longing, I raise my left hand to caress the form as if I were caressing her cheek. We sing together and then I say, "Mother, does this mean I will be with you soon?" It seems odd because we are together in that*

> *moment. She laughs lightly and continues singing in a reassuring way.*
>
> *Unexpectedly, I find myself transported to another dream scene in which I open the window in my room so that I can go flying among the autumnal leaves, which I do for some time, weaving in and out of the treetops. Normally I don't do such things in lucid dreams, but I feel like having fun and celebrating. Then I awake.*

Hearing my mother's finely tuned voice puts me in touch with the many-layered memories of sitting next to her in church. Then, neither of us could have imagined our love for God and for one another would be shared in this way. This pivotal dream meeting felt a culmination of all the dreams that had come before, one in which we could at last know one another as beloved Beings of Light, the same light that illumines Creation in love.

Finally, the lucid dream comes full circle, returns me to the bedroom of my London flat, and, in sheer pleasure, I take flight, soaring over London, free from all constraints, confident the charity would raise the needed funds, and certain in the knowledge that love is eternal.

Celestial Cities

I need to give some context for the next dream, "The Emerald City", which begins in the gardens of Sir Richard Branson's house, a person I have not met and a place I have never been. However, I should explain that the counselling center Help, which I directed for several years, was started as a free student helpline by Branson some forty years before. My role as Director had been to oversee the organization's transition into a fully-fledged affordable counselling center and self-sustaining charity, independent of its parent organization.

With the support of the active board of trustees, led by a valiant Chair, [12] and many dedicated volunteers, this aim was eventually achieved but, at the time of this dream, we were in the throes of bringing the center into line with charitable status requirements, expanding the service and raising additional funding.

Although I was in my forties, the undertaking put me in touch with the energy and enthusiasm of my mid-twenties, when I helped establish the English Department of a newly founded Teacher Training College in Poland, soon after the country had gained its freedom from Soviet rule. At the time of this dream, the Help Board had been appealing to Branson for more time and support. So, it is perhaps unsurprising that a dream Being appears who I initially mistake for Branson.

The opening garden scene includes a second more prosaic image, that of my father working on the engine of a second-hand, 1975 Volkswagen Rabbit — our family car during my late teens and early twenties. This car became the stuff of family legend. Bought for its gas-efficient engine during a fuel hike, buying the Rabbit had been a strictly more-for-your-money purchase as the hard upholstery, manual windows, and cramped quarters testified. No matter how many times the Rabbit overheated or how much fixing the car's engine required, my dad always thought he'd got a good deal!

The car's license plate displayed the letters "PCP", the initials of an illicit recreational drug in the early 1980s. Mom and Dad didn't know about the drug's popular usage when they bought the car. Other drivers, thinking my mom was a drug dealer, tried to get her to pull over. Mom, who was in her fifties, would have none of it and got the license plate changed.

Unbelievably, she ended up with the ID of the fictional British secret agent James Bond, 007. [13] When teenage boys and grown men driving behind the Rabbit saw my mom's shimmering blonde hair through the car's back window, they couldn't resist honking at her. Even so, Mom decided to keep the license plate. She said it gave her a perverse satisfaction when young men pulled up alongside of her only to see they were honking at a grandmother. She and I celebrated when, one night, the car got stolen and smashed up beyond repair by a young man high on drugs, who took the car for a joyride — and fortunately survived the crash unharmed.

I associate the Rabbit's appearance in the dream with my own struggle to streamline the counselling center and my fear that all our efforts to "fix" the situation might yet end with the center's closure. That night, before falling asleep, I had been singing my prayers and asking for God's help:

> *The dream begins in what appears to be Richard Branson's back garden, where my mother and I are walking together arm in arm. At the back of the garden, much to my surprise, my father tinkers with the engine of our family car, a Volkswagen Rabbit. From the right, three small animals approach my mother. One is a baby llama, which seems very odd to me. "What is a llama doing here?" I wonder. Another animal comes from behind and bites at my left fingers playfully. Looking down, I see it is a baby goat. A beautiful black and white calf then catches my attention and I call to my mother, "Mama, look at the calf!"*
>
> *Suddenly I find myself in Branson's bedroom, where a man is sleeping. He wakes up when I enter and looks as surprised to see me as I am to see him. Nonetheless, he lifts the bedcovers invitingly. Drawing near the bed, I can tell that although he looks very like Branson, he differs in his youth and luminous countenance.*
>
> *The desire to make love with this angelic man overcomes me, but with this feeling also comes lucidity, and I ask him, "Do you know this is a dream?" Although I don't want the dream to end, I acquiesce to the pull of the winds that carry me off at tremendous speed into the formless Black Light before the man can respond.*

It later struck me that the dream had seemingly gone to great lengths to spark my lucid state by presenting one vivid image after another: the llama's exotic presence, the goat's playful bite, and the calf's striking beauty, each focusing my attention differently. The animals spoke to me of an instinctive, almost magical, energy, one that would help me bear my responsibilities.

However, I only became lucid after entering "Branson's" bedroom, which was pervaded by a sense of the rejuvenating power of Eros — a life-giving, creative force. However, when I reluctantly "let go" of my attachment to the dream scenario and the idea of physical union, I intuitively recognized that this desire sprang from a yearning for a greater, more universal love. As if in response, the dreamscape dissolved as the energy of the Black Light carried me swiftly away:

When the movement slows, I begin to see spirals of golden light around me. I exclaim, "Well, this is a new form!" The beauty and playfulness of the spirals reminds me of Leonardo DaVinci's studies of spirals, and I wonder if he had ever visited this place. But the thought goes by in a flash as I am set down on black, sparkling sands.

Two unseen Beings lead me to a high viewpoint. Below, a vast city of magnificent buildings and gardens shines forth in shades of green. One part of me thinks, "The Emerald City!", while another exclaims, "Oh no, it can't really be!" But there it is, wondrously spread before me.

I say silently, "Take me there!" and suddenly my soul is carried towards the city. In my eagerness, I realize that my thoughts have a grasping quality. With this subtle shift in consciousness, the scene before me changes. In an instant, I am back in the bedroom where the lucid dream began, only now in the bed, and apparently waking up from sleep!

Still in the same dream, I worry that I have overslept and missed my appointment in the waking world with a friend, who had been planning to come by that morning around 9:00 am. Since there isn't a clock to be seen in the room, I stumble to the reception in Branson's house and ask the woman there to call my friend. The receptionist reassures me, "It's only 7:00!" Feeling exhausted, I return to the bedroom and go back to sleep, the dream finally ending with my actual alarm ringing and waking me at 7:30 am.

Much as this dream begins with my mother's guiding presence supporting me, the end of the dream brings me to wakefulness with motherly care. I'm so grateful I was given more time to sleep in the dream! The framing of the lucid dream feels appropriate to the magical visions of light it displayed, first of the golden spirals and then a celestial city, in what Sufi mystics would call the "Celestial Earth", a place beyond time and space where all forms are revealed as Holy light.

In lucidity, my mind had initially tried to make sense of the dream vision recalling the "Emerald City" of the novel *The Wonderful Wizard of Oz* and popularized in the film of 1939. [14] The film made a powerful impression on my generation because it was one of the first black and white films to introduce color, in this case the magical colors of the "land of Oz". I still remember watching the film for the first time in the late 1960's and feeling awed by the sudden blaze of green light surrounding the city of Oz.

Yet this immediate association was eclipsed by the sheer

beauty of the cityscape and gardens of my dream. I sensed that in this lucid place, all Beings knew themselves as one with the Light and acted in accordance with the Beauty and Truth in the Light. (In later lucid dreams, I was to be introduced to some of the luminous inhabitants of this world and to visit their resplendent gardens.)

As I recall this dream now, it occurs to me that perhaps my mother wanted to show me the magnificent city where she now resides. I also sense the relationship of the "earthly" garden in which the dream begins to the "celestial" gardens of light, the former being where we live and express our full humanity, the latter revealing the dazzling truth that we are more than we know. Finally, the lucid dream gave me confidence that the counselling center was in bigger hands than mine and that grace would account for what efficiency, fundraising, and time could not. And so it proved to be.

Gifts of the Spirit

A few months after my vision of the Emerald City, the New Year began with me feeling weakened and emptied from my work and a prolonged illness. It had been some while since I had truly spent time in prayer, so on the night of this next lucid dream, "The Gifts of the Spirit", I repeated the Holy names of Elohim and Jesus slowly while breathing deeply.

As I drifted off to sleep, my soul slipped seamlessly onto a still, silent expanse of Black Light. A sacred song spontaneously arose in me and as I sang, a powerful ecstasy filled me, imparting the energy required for the day ahead. After some time, the dream continued with my being once again set down on sparkling sands. This time, however, the sands formed a golden circle covered by a dome of radiant darkness:

> *In the center of this golden circle, on a rock, there stands a crystal cup. Instinctively, I know it is for me. Taking it in my hands, I notice how beautiful and youthful my hands look, unmarked by weather or age. The Sufi teaching that the hands express the heart suddenly makes sense to me. The cup contains a string of pearls, and I am reminded of the string of pearls my mother had in waking life; but these pearls shine with a wondrous luminescence.*

Although my mother does not figure directly in this dream, the pearls immediately brought her to mind. Her pearl necklace was the one expensive necklace that she owned. She wore her pearls only on Sundays and special occasions. When she took the pearls out of their case, she would eye them appreciatively before clasping them around her lovely throat. The pearls accentuated her quiet elegance. When she sang in church, they rose and fell with her breath, and so I connect the pearls with the sound of her soulful voice.

My mother had got my dad to buy her the pearls during the early days of their marriage, in those heady times when my father was a dentist stationed in Okinawa with the US Airforce and before my eldest brother was born, a time when the world was truly their "oyster". After her death, I inherited her pearls, though I rarely wore them.

In my thirties, I learned that my mother's pearls were cultured, not natural, yet they remained priceless to me. For my mother, they signified a luxurious extravagance for which she longed. As I now understand this lucid dream, the dream-pearls signify both the fullness of my mother's love and the abundant riches of the inner world — Jesus's "pearl of great price", of such beauty and worth that one gives all to have:

> *Then I notice that the crystal cup holds other objects. First, three pairs of silver earrings tumble out into my hand: one of small stars, and two of topaz stones, one set with a square base, and the other, a round one. These last two pairs are like earrings of mine in waking life but of much finer quality. There is also a slim, rectangular bottle of golden perfume. The thought, "How well you know me!" fills my heart. I am speaking to God for I am quietly certain these are God's*

gifts to me.

When I put on the star earrings, my fingertips feel alive to the delicacy of their design — one of the few times in a lucid dream that the sense of touch has felt so real.

Now I become curious about the perfume. The golden perfume catches the light as I raise the bottle. When I spray it on my neck, beads of perfume spread out in a fine mist. The beauty of its touch and fragrance nearly overwhelms me. I am afraid I'll lose my equilibrium and be taken out of lucidity, but then the impact softens. What is this fragrance? Words fall short, but it can be likened to the pure pine-laden air of high mountains in winter or the sage-laden air of the of the high deserts at first light. I relax and surrender to the fragrance's beauty.

The exclamation I made on receiving the gifts, "How well you know me", speaks of my consciousness that the pearl necklace, delicate earrings, and perfume were gifts of the Spirit. Each piece of jewelry resonated with qualities of the Spirit yet, at the same time, each resounded with personal nuances linked to my human experience.

The topaz blue and silver of the earrings, a favorite combination of mine, signify transcendence, a communion with Beauty beyond words. I associate topaz blue with my mother's soul. She had a gold ring with a large gemstone of this color, which she kept in a blue velvet case. As with her pearls, I believed it was a real gem, although as I learned in my fifties when a local jeweler valued the stone, it was in fact costume jewelry. Nonetheless, the color of the stone lost none of its luster for me.

In the dream, I knew the earrings of topaz and silver had been crafted to help me listen for the soul's beauty in words and in silence. The perfume blended the scents of Nature that had put me in touch with the Spirit during my childhood — accents of desert sage and mountain pines.

The bottle of perfume reminded me of my mother. Mindful that she had a family of five to feed on a limited budget each month, she did allow herself one extravagant purchase, a perfume called "Youth dew". The small-waisted perfume bottle, with its trademark gold bow around it, always evoked for me a mysterious feminine presence, heavy with the freshness of oakmoss, the elegant scent of iris, and the spicy warmth of nutmeg and cinnamon.

My mother only applied the perfume once she had completed her morning toilette. She would stand at the bathroom mirror, tilt her head to the left, place her left hand lightly on her right breast and spray the perfume onto her neck. When she did so, it felt as if the droplets hovered in the air before gently falling like dew upon the two of us. Her movements had the ritual significance of a biblical anointing. After she left a room, the scent of her perfume lingered in the air as a reminder of her presence.

Mom wore this perfume all her adult life, remaining loyal to the same Estée Lauder brand. The morning she died, I prepared her body for burial by covering her in a mist of her perfume before the undertakers carted her away. Thereafter, her perfume bottle served as a tangible reminder of her invisible presence. From time to time, I would take off the cap just to breathe in my mother's love even though, as with her pearls, I rarely wore her perfume.

Reflecting on the meaning of this lucid dream, I felt that the Spirit had given me my own living scent to wear in the world, my own path to follow, so different from my mother's on the earthly plane yet so intimately entwined on the spiritual. All these layered blends of association within the dream became articulated in this moment.

Returning to the dream and to its conclusion:

After I have spent some time breathing in the perfume's scent, a strong wind begins to pull at me. The tug of the winds tells me that it is time to "go back". By now, however, I am unsure where I have come from! I raise my arms over my head to signal my willingness to return and instantly my soul is carried by an invisible Being on the dark phosphorescence. At one point, we pass through what appears to be the edge of a vast black cube, the blackness of which stands out against the bright darkness.

I begin to feel somehow stuck or claustrophobic. This feeling goes on for some time, until I relax and become curious about how I will come out of such a deep lucid dream. I am so very grateful for it as I now feel ready to continue with my life's work. For some while, I stay in this "holding space" until the alarm wakes me up.

The gratitude aroused by the dream permeated my waking life. The gifts given, as with those presented by the three Wise Men to the infant Jesus, affirmed for me that each person comes into the world bearing gifts of the Spirit. This reassurance helped me to trust in the abiding, intimate love of Spirit, love that falls like a fragrant essence upon the world.

Part Three
Lessons in Grace

One More

So far, my focus has been on sharing what my dreams of my mother have taught me. In giving a context to the dreams, I have needed to describe my family life as well. Nearly nine years after my mother's death, my father died unexpectedly, just a few months after my dream of the "Pearl of Great Price". It feels as if the gifts I received in that dream strengthened me in advance of this sudden loss. Given the family dynamics that have resonated throughout these pages, I would like to share what happened to my father after my mother's death and to relate the one lucid dream in which he appeared to me in the days leading up to his own death.

A year after my mom passed away, my father moved from California to North Carolina to live in the townhouse where he and Mom had planned to spend their last years together, near my brother Carey and his young family. Dad told me that when he got to North Carolina and unpacked the boxes of Mom's frying pans, he broke down sobbing on the kitchen floor. When I mentioned this to Mom's eldest sister, she said, "Serves him right, the son of a bitch." Yet, I have no doubt Dad's heart was softened by losing Mom and that he regretted not having fully appreciated her more, consequently forfeiting love that he could have known more deeply.

Some weeks before Mom died, she had sat Dad and me down for a talk to say that Dad wasn't the kind of man to be alone and that he should remarry soon after her death.

Evidently, Dad took Mom at her word because less than a year after her death, he announced his intention to marry again. Before doing so, he travelled to London to visit me for the first time in the twenty-five years I had been living in Europe.

He had come to tell me in person that he'd met a lady and wasn't the kind of man to be alone, so he was going to re-marry, if that was okay. "That's alright Dad," I replied, "Mom always said you should re-marry if something happened to her." It surprised me that it mattered to him at all what I thought and that he would come so far to tell me his plans. "You see," he added, "I like sex." "That makes sense to me, Dad," I said, "I like sex too." Having married my mother only six months after meeting her so they could sleep together, fifty years on, he was about to marry a woman already in her sixties, after a similarly brief courtship. Dad added that she was a Southern lady, a church-going one at that; in a small town that's how it was, and besides, he loved her.

Even though he hadn't yet told me who was his wife-to-be, I knew. She was the first person from the local church to bring food over when the family and I were caring for my dying mother at Carey's home in North Carolina. Her name was Susan, and when I opened the front door for her, and saw her for the first time, she reminded me of Mom, sweet, svelte, sophisticated, and a bit sad. When Dad came to London to tell me he would be marrying a second time, I guessed correctly that his future wife would be Susan.

Dad met Susan at the church that my brother Carey and his family attended. As had been the case with Mom, Susan sang in the choir and taught in the Sunday school. Not long after meeting her, Dad even got baptized.

As the story goes, Susan had spotted my father sitting in the congregation with the family when she was singing in the choir and asked her sister "Who is that handsome man?" When Dad went on a Seniors' bus trip with church members to a nearby tourist site, he ended up sitting next to Susan on the bus. She later confessed to me that she had pulled some strings with her friend to get the seat next to Dad.

After their wedding, Dad took Susan to some of the National Parks where we used to go as a family, landscapes that had expanded our view beyond the confines of suburbia — the Grand Canyon, Yosemite, and the Mojave Desert. Dad tried to get Susan to stay in a tent, but she vetoed the idea, so after that they stayed in hotels. He showed her his family's old farmhouse in Ogden, Utah, which the US government had seized for military purposes back in 1942, paying little in reparation and thereby establishing Dad's lifelong distrust of the government. Susan, who had spent thirty years running a local farm with her first husband, could understand how hard that must have been for Dad. Together, they visited the kind of places Mom had always longed to go, especially London, where I lived, and then taking a cruise ship along the Alaskan coast.

Susan had five good years with Dad before the onset of his dementia, but by the time they came to visit me to London, his impairment plainly showed. After asking me the date for the tenth time, he would go up to a stranger and say, "Hey there, could you tell me something? What's the date?" He constantly fretted about missing the flight back. But the old Dad showed through when visiting the National Gallery. Pointing up towards a painting by Raphael, he gravely said to the attendant: "Excuse me, sir, how do they manage to change all those light bulbs way up there?"

With Susan, Dad opened his heart to life's simple pleasures, becoming a reformed character. The estrogen his doctor's prescribed to keep his prostate cancer under control made him more tender, while dementia tempered his irascibility, apart from which Susan demanded the respect owed to her and would not put up with any of Dad's temperamental nonsense.

On our family's behalf, Carey managed Dad's accounts and took on the unenviable task of telling Dad he wasn't allowed to drive anymore. Given Dad's love of driving and the many miles he had driven over the years, we all feared the moment Carey asked for his car keys. But Dad placed the keys in Carey's open palm with a shrug of his shoulders. After that, Dad would say, "You'd better watch the speed limit in this town, or the police will take your car keys away!"

Dad surprised us all by growing old with style and grace. He got himself a hat to which he proudly affixed buttons that celebrated "senior moments" and he attached his wallet to a chain on his belt so he wouldn't lose it. To keep focused, he developed a routine: rising at 4:00am to go to the gym for an hour, spending the rest of the morning going through the mail, followed by lunch, a nap, and an afternoon trip to pick up another stapler, clock, roll of tape, pair of scissors or notepad from the local shop to replace the ones he invariably mislaid.

Dad put yellow post-it notes up everywhere as reminders of what he needed to do, including notes to remind him about the notes. When Carey came over, he'd go into Dad's office to unstick the slips of paper from Dad's computer monitor, bookshelves, and phone and throw them away. Dad never noticed.

When I was yet a child, Dad told me that when he "got old with spittle on his chin", he'd kill himself. Instead, as he entered his eighties, he talked about how life felt "pretty sweet" and how he liked to sit in the sun and have a coffee or hold Susan's hand. All the same, while Dad was slowly dementing, Carey spent hours searching for Dad's missing M1 Carbine rifle, afraid Dad might use it, accidentally or intentionally. After Dad died, Susan's nine-year old grandson showed us where the gun was — in the hall closet, loaded! The only belonging of Dad's that Carey wanted was the M1. He had it cleaned and mounted. "That rifle almost blew my foot off," he said, "It's mine now."

Susan always made a point of saying to my brothers and me, "Boy, your dad loves you." Whenever she said so, we kept quiet. To deflect her attention from our recriminating silence, I finally took to saying, "And he really loves you Susan," pleased to see her smile wistfully. Later, I would say, "Yes, and I loved him too." It struck me that by then Dad had made peace with himself and life, even befriending his two worst enemies: old age and vulnerability. Meantime, my brothers and I were struggling to come to terms with the New Dad.

On the phone to me in London, he would go through the usual round of questions, "Where are you?" "What are you doing?" The answers never made any sense to him even when he remembered them: "London? That's far away, isn't it? It's cold there, isn't it?" "Poland? That's cold too, isn't it?" "Directing a counselling center? What's that?" To me, it always felt that what he was really asking was: "Why did you have to leave home and not come back?" I didn't feel able to give an answer, but I remember the last time Mom had asked me why I didn't return to the States to live near them. She and I were sitting in her car at a building supply shop near my parents' home. I said to her, "Mom, you know I can't do that with Dad." In response, she opened her mouth and let out a long scream as we drove out of the parking lot.

The New Dad said things that made me wonder what had possessed me to make a life so far from home such as, "I can't remember much facts-wise, but I remember the sound of your voice" or "It's good to hear your voice. I love you. Want you to know that." He had never talked that way before.

When Carey called to tell me that Dad had pancreatic cancer and had only a few months to live, the news shocked us all. We had been concerned about his low-grade prostate cancer and were wondering how we would deal with his Alzheimer's. In the oncologist's waiting room, Dad complained about the heels of his shoes wearing down. "Time for a new pair," Carey observed. "Well," Dad intoned, "Might want to wait on that, don't think I'll be needing a new pair."

As it happened, Dad lived only three weeks after the diagnosis. Whether it was his dementia or wishful thinking, he couldn't remember that he had been diagnosed with cancer and kept saying to the doctor, "I'm sure that stomachache is from something I ate." In the hospital he repeatedly thanked the staff for taking such good care of an old man, endearing himself to the nurses. "Doctor Ziemer," they'd say to Carey, "Isn't your father the sweetest man!" Carey just smiled.

I made it to Dad's side just three nights before he died. It was a lucid dream I have called "Come Home" that compelled me to catch the flight to North Carolina right away:

> *In the dream, I am climbing down a steep rocky slope on a clear, sunny day in the Sierra Nevada Mountains of California. An unseen man takes my hand to help me down. With surprise, I recognize it is my father's hand. The familiarity of his presence strikes me powerfully as his hand touches mine. He sits down silently next to me.*
>
> *The moment has such reality that I become lucid and say to him, "I know this is a dream, but I do not want to leave your side". It feels as if we are truly together, so I stay with him and tell him how much I love him, how he must know that, and how I know he loves me. He remains silent, looking at me with intense concentration and love. While speaking, I begin to cry and awake from the dream in tears.*

It turned out that during this same night, Dad's kidneys failed. By the time I got to his bedside two days later, he could hardly move and wasn't able to speak. Alone with him in the darkened room, as in the dream, I told him what an amazing man he was, and how I was proud to have him for a father, grateful for what he'd given me, and that he must know I loved him. A large tear slipped down his cheek. It was the first time we had ever cried together.

Steve, who had borne the brunt of Dad's violent rages as a child, came out to be with Dad in his final days. The night of Dad's passing, after Susan and the rest of the family had gone home, Steve and I sang hymns and prayed by our father's bedside. Dad died a few minutes after midnight, with Steve singing to accompany him as he passed over, while I stroked his forehead.

After Dad's death, we cleaned out his office, where we came upon signs that his dementia had progressed more than we knew. To occupy himself, Dad had taken to cutting out magazine advertisements related to his interests, meticulously filing them all away. There were two large filing cabinets full of clippings for computer accessories, camping gear, fishing equipment and various life insurance policies. He had also cut his address out of every piece of mail he got, filing these away too. Dad had always been terrified of having his identity stolen, yet he couldn't have known that the dementia had already robbed him of much of it.

We also discovered that Dad had also been the victim of scams. We came across dozens of checks that he had written to bogus charities or sweepstakes but had forgotten to send. Subsequently, we found out that he had given away nearly a hundred-thousand dollars to fraudsters!

Dad's last email was to a woman abroad, to whom it seems he had been sending money. In just a few lines, he had written his own eulogy, "I grew up on a farm in Utah, went to dental school in San Francisco and worked as a dentist for forty-seven years. My wife of forty-nine years died a few years ago and I thought life was over, but I met a nice woman and we've been happy. You never know how things will work out so hang in there." I noticed he hadn't mentioned his children.

While sorting out Dad's office, a few family keepsakes were unearthed: an old black and white wedding photo of him and Mom tucked away in a drawer; pictures of his mother with her parents camping out in the covered wagon they rode from Utah to Yellowstone National Park; colored slides from the early years with Mom in Okinawa, Japan; his arrowhead necklace; his Swiss army knife; and the embossed stamp he used to mark his letters that read, "W. A. Ziemer, D.D.S., Inc.", standing for Walther Alexander Ziemer, Doctor of Dental Surgery, Incorporated.

My brothers and I also came across the long-lost retirement scrapbook his dental staff had made, full of their fondness for him. They had written notes to thank him for his advice and concern, all that he had taught them, and how he'd been like a father to them. His clients had thanked him for his good work and for being a dentist they could trust. They shared how much they enjoyed hearing about his camping exploits. Their words helped me see Dad from another angle.

We found Dad's wall safe wide open and stacked full of expired life insurance policies, his newly renewed passport, and a copy of his will. Before moving to North Carolina, he'd managed to squirrel away some money from selling the family home on Garfield Street during the boom days of California real-estate — the best financial investment he ever made. He had often talked about wanting to leave my brothers and me some money. We were hoping there would be enough to cover the nursing care we thought he was going to need for his

Alzheimer's.

A few days following Dad's funeral, Susan told me that after being romanced by my dad, no one else would ever do for her. I thought that would make Mom smile. Dad's virility remained vital to him to the end. Among the books on his shelf, I found *Sex After Sixty*, while Carey uncovered boxes of Viagra in the attic.

There is a saying that life is not a dress rehearsal. Yet it felt to me that in his last years, Dad was given a second chance at happiness and that he made the best of it. He got to know his new wife's family and friends, joining in their family reunions and barbecues, and without the pressures of running a business and making ends meet, found the happiness that had always eluded him with our family.

Dad's funeral ended up feeling more like a wedding, with what Southerners call a "visitation" line, a long queue of many family, friends and acquaintances who had numerous fond anecdotes to recall about Dad, what a character he was and what they remembered about him: his imposing form walking down the street, the stories he told about his camping days, his cheerful greetings at the gym, or the way he hand-fertilized his tomato plants with a toothbrush (since most all the bees in North Carolina had been killed off by pesticides). His cantankerousness had softened sufficiently enough to become part of his legendary charm.

At Dad's funeral, my brother Steve gave a heartfelt talk about what made Dad great in God's eyes. He started out by saying, "My dad wasn't a happy man when I was growing up...." Carey and I tensed up at those words, fearing the worst, and were greatly relieved when they were followed by Steve's eulogy to the happiness Dad had discovered after he'd had his heart "broken open" by Mom's death. During the reception that followed, there was even a slideshow of his life played to his favorite song, Frank Sinatra's "I Did it My Way".

Upon his deathbed, aged eighty-three and just hours before he died, Dad lay there comatose. Susan leaned over to give him a final kiss goodbye. To our surprise, with his eyes still closed, he said his last words, "One more!" So, she kissed him again. I like to think he would have said the same to my mother and that she would have kissed him too.

New Light

The following two dreams bear witness to the adage that "mistakes are our teachers; they help us to learn".[15] Both dreams took place during the springtime, and both bear the mark of the confusion that filled my personal life at the time, the ninth year on from my mother's passing. The contrast between the messiness of my life and the beauty of the spring reminds me now of the T. S. Eliot line, "April is the cruelest month." Nevertheless, the dreams imparted the light of understanding.

By the time of the first dream, "The Open Window", I had learned that windows in dreams signify a new outlook on the world in waking life — the larger the window, the more expansive the perspective. Similarly, I had come to appreciate that an open window in a dream can represent an openness to the Spirit, shown as light and air, the clear glass intimating that the ego has become transparent to the Divine. In this dream, however, lucidity eludes me:

My mother and I are inside a charming country church on a sunny afternoon. Warm light shines through the windows to my right. As we approach the altar, a strong wind blows one of the windows open and shut repeatedly with a loud banging sound. When I try to shut the window, the wind catches it and pulls the latch out of my hands. Each time, I try to push against the window to close it, the wind

> *drives the window open, forcing me back. This makes me increasingly frantic and fearful. The struggle continues until my agitation wakes me up, breathing heavily from the effort in the dream.*

Upon waking, I understood that my determination to shut the window mirrored an inward resistance to letting in the light of Spirit. My mind, preoccupied with shutting the window, failed to see what it already knew: first, that my mother was no longer alive and second, that the wind was Spirit, attempting to gain my attention by making its presence known with increasing forcefulness. Willfulness and fearfulness hindered my apprehension. The stronger the wind, the more I resisted. My preoccupation with shutting the window kept lucidity at bay.

The lucid dream that followed two months later, "New Light", magnifies the theme of letting in the light.[16] In this dream, my mother is noticeably absent, as she no longer inhabits her bedroom where I would have expected to find her, and her belongings have been removed. My surprise at this brings lucidity:

> *I stand outside the family home where I grew up on Garfield Street. Entering the house, I go straight to the room that belonged to my mother in her later years. There, I am surprised to see that the lovely furnishings have been taken away and that two of my nieces sleep on mattresses on the floor, as if they have just moved in. Startled by this, I become lucid and say, "You wouldn't be here. This must be a dream."*

My mental state feels muddled, so I say, "Okay God, what next then?" Slowly the dreamscape falls away and my soul is carried into glittering darkness a great distance. Eventually, rows of crystal hexagonal structures, like in a honeycomb, form a vast tunnel through which my soul descends at an incredible speed. Far away a speck of light shows up where the tunnel opens to an unknown destination.

Finally, the movement stops, and it feels as if my body rests on Holy ground, in a fetal position on my right side. The omnipresent darkness lies heavily over me like a thick blanket, bringing complete surrender. A part of me thinks, "I guess life knows I need this."

Suddenly, a dome of morning light rises around and through me. This light feels pure, full of all of life, including the sky, trees, birds, the earth, and my soul. The light has a musicality like spring waters bubbling or a gentle wind amongst leaves. I think for a moment that I've awakened to a sunny spring day and that I must be hearing sounds from outside. But then I understand the experience to be my awakening to what light truly is, and all that it creates and contains. Like an apple on a grassy field, I rest in the light until the alarm wakes me up, feeling clear-headed and refreshed, like Nature newborn in spring.

In this dream, the light, rather than coming from without or within, infused everything all at once, as if the light itself had conceived all life, including my mother's and my own.

Where was my mother in this dream? Not in her room,

which had been emptied to make way for a new generation, nor in her grave, which had been emptied by time, but in the light that everywhere gives birth to life through love.

Enveloped in Love

Eight months after my father's passing, my day job had steadily taken over my life as I sought financial support for the charitable center I was directing. Many hours of filling out funding applications on the computer had taken a toll — pain in my neck gradually took hold of me and medication failed to relieve it.

On the home front, my then husband had been away for weeks, and I was now preparing for an upcoming move on my own. Packing accentuated the pain. Only taking time off, deep tissue massages and gentle yoga eased the discomfort.

During the weeks I'd been on pain-relief medication, my dreams had ceased. However, a few nights after coming off the medicine, I awoke in the early hours of the night and felt the desire to pray again. My mother did not appear in the lucid dream that ensued, but I share it here because it prefigures her presence in the dreams that followed.

Having sung the Lord's Prayer three times, I found myself dreaming about a counsellor from my work who was having money troubles and whom I was trying to help. Discerning that the dream reflected my own fundraising concerns, I became lucid and had the dream "Black Lace Light":

Without hesitation, I walk to a nearby window and dive out into emptiness. As I fall, I call out for the Holy Spirit to come for me. After a long descent, my willful approach to leaping into the unknown becomes apparent to me. Recalling the words with which Jesus rebuked Satan when Satan tempted him to leap off a cliff, "Thou shall not tempt the Lord thy God", I feel chastened and exclaim, "Well, I didn't mean it quite that way God!"

Immediately, a strong wind seizes my soul and carries me on. Suddenly, I am transported, as if breaking through the surface of the sea, into a blazing blue sky. "The blue!" I think, reassured by memories of blue light in other dreams, for me a color of spiritual inspiration. This blue seems the most dazzling yet. Crossing the endless blue light takes time and feels like a cleansing. Another descent into iridescent blackness follows.

The descent ends in a black whirling cloud made of what seems to be veil upon veil of black lace with moonlight shining through. My soul knows that it is at the very center of things, in God's embrace. The spinning cloud's lacy forms are exquisitely intricate, yet simple and beautiful. Their beauty is irresistible, and I lift my right hand to touch the cloud. Doing so fills me with great joy, an unbounded trust, and a profound knowing. The lacy pattern reads like a hieroglyph for life, a secret text in Braille for life's coding. A wonderful mysterious love, full of grace, envelops me.

Then, my soul is taken out of the lacy cloud and carried back "home" on velvety darkness. An intense ecstasy ebbs through me all the long journey back to my waking life. Upon waking, I feel very tired, grateful, and immensely encouraged.

This lucid dream acted like balm on my physical and emotional exhaustion, and my neck pain lessened.

I associate the lacey light with a dress that I bought in my early twenties on a shopping trip with my mother. At that time, attracted by the warmth and romance of the culture, I was studying Spanish and learning Flamenco dancing. The dress, an extravagance for me, was made of hand-woven lace, a testimony to the time and labor involved in its creation. Such a gown, with its subtle floral pattern, represented the elegance of old-world Spain replete with human and Divine eros, a rare find.

When I first put the dress on, my mother's approving eyes, reflected in the dressing room mirror, told me that she would have enjoyed wearing the dress to the dinners, concerts and plays that she herself had so longed to attend. Over the next thirty years, I would wear the dress only a dozen or so times on special occasions. However, in this dream of the whirling cloud of Black Light lace, a far greater intimate splendor was disclosed, for my soul knew itself to be part of the fabric of the universe.

A few weeks after this dream, during the Easter holiday, I went to join my husband in Warsaw, Poland, where he had been working for many weeks. With my neck still sore and feeling very tired, I slept late and had a dream, [17] one that paralleled the previous imagery of "Black Lace Light" but more concerned with my personal relationships:

In the dream, I dress to attend a wedding where there will be a man I long to love, though as yet unknown to me. A wall-size mirror reveals that I am dressed in a form-fitting black lace body suit with no undergarments! Above all, I am moved by the strange beauty of this outfit on me. It fits extraordinarily well; in fact, it seems the bodysuit has been sewn onto me, making for a strange combination of sensuality, innocence, and refined beauty. I feel beautiful in this black lace and comfortable in it.

Yet rather than becoming lucid at the beauty of the dress or of the mirror catching the soft golden lights of the room lamps, I become preoccupied with my preparations for the wedding. It crosses my mind that wearing black doesn't seem appropriate for a wedding and that others may find my clothing immodest. However, it doesn't occur to me that I can take the outfit off.

I put on a pair of black undergarments over the lace to cover myself. As this only heightens the sensuality, I decide instead to wear an elegant black skirt to tone down the sexiness of the black lace.

I then drive to the seaside in a sky-blue Volkswagen bug of the 1970's to pick up my mother. The sea runs along the road to my right. Pitch-black waves with frothy crests of white rise vertically, curving slightly before tumbling straight down at the edge of the shore. I recognize these waves as reminiscent of the black cloud of lacy light from the previous dream but remain preoccupied with worrying that my mother, who is standing on the shore, may get swamped by a wave (forgetting that she has passed away). At this moment, a bugle, played on the street outside my bedroom window, awakens me!

Hearing the bugle's call, I knew the hour must be late, as it sounded out every morning at 11:15 from the Royal Castle's clock tower to mark the first bomb that fell on Warsaw in World War II, destroying the tower. This dream and the historical associations with the clarion call sounded foreboding. I sensed there and then that the dream presaged dramatic change in my own life but could not imagine that before long, my husband and I would be divorced. It struck me later that the powerful waves and the bugle's cry were attempting to wake me up to a truth I could not yet face.

At the time of having this dream, I noticed only that its imagery comprised a form-based representation of the previous, more abstract lucid dream. For instance, the lacy dark cloud of the initial lucid dream was now represented by the foamy, black waves, and the unbounded blue light that had transported me in that dream manifested in this one as a sky-blue car.

I felt disappointed that my preoccupation with my own appearance in the dream and my fear of the waves kept me from becoming lucid. Nonetheless, in retrospect, it's clear to me that this dream also foretold the wedding that would take place five years later, when I would truly marry for love and, in doing so, marry up with my creative expression.

Together, these two dreams heralded the need for me to stop fearing the unknown and to live more soulfully the creative fullness of life that my mother and I each so desired, enriched by both spiritual and human intimacy and love. The shimmering void depicted in the imagery of waves and lacy veils of layered darkness empowered me to move forward into life, covered in grace and secure in the knowledge that I would not be alone.

Where Heaven and Earth Touch

Nearly ten years and numerous lucid dreams on from my mother's death, and in response to dream guidance "to share the dreams", I began to tell others about my dreams in more public forums. The presentations, workshops, and writings produced during the decade that followed eventually coalesced into two books, *The Hidden Lives of Dreams* and *Lucid Surrender*.[18] I knew that I must honor the dream guidance and articulate what I had learned from Lucid Surrender — a process that continues to this day.

Doing so lightened the burden of my professional responsibilities at the counselling center, where, with the help of a dedicated board of trustees and many devoted volunteers, we were moving towards becoming a registered charity — no small feat given the financial and administrative hurdles. My nightly dreams fueled my work by day in an astounding reciprocity, giving me the guidance and the confidence needed to actualize the shared vision for the center.

Throughout, my mother's presence in my dreams encouraged me, and I found myself wondering whether she now regarded my domestic circumstances at this time differently from when she had been alive. Then the minister of our family church had reminded her that in marrying my father she had taken an oath before God and therefore should stay with him no matter the personal cost. Mom had said as much to me more than once concerning my own marital unhappiness. Her personal story, as she told it to me, helps to explain why.

In 1952, at the age of twenty-five, my mother left her rainy hometown of Seattle, Washington hoping for a new life and clearer skies in California — the "Golden State". In the same year, then aged twenty-two, Dad left behind the cold winters and desert nights of Ogden, Utah, hoping for the same. Dad went on to study dentistry at the University of California San Francisco while Mom began working at the university hospital as a nurse. Both were shocked to find out that the weather in San Francisco, located in Northern California, was cold and damp for much of the year! When they crossed paths in 1955, both were craving sunshine and love.

Dad was a patient at the hospital when he met my mother, who was working on the surgical ward. He'd just had his hernia repaired, and she had the job of giving him penicillin shots in his rear end every few hours. Dad felt mortified at having to bare his bottom to a curvaceous, blonde nurse.

When my mother came to give him the injections, she hardly smiled because she'd recently been in a car accident in which a couple of her front teeth got knocked out against the dashboard. She was surprised when Dad took an interest in her broken teeth. He begged her to let him work on them for his dental school practicum, promising to make her a dental bridge to replace the gaps in her smile. He also asked her to go out on a date.

She accepted the offer to have the bridge made, but the first time Dad asked her out, she flatly refused, saying that nurses weren't allowed to date patients. Although she had noticed his good looks, she claimed she felt too exhausted from long hours on the ward to have any romantic thoughts about him. Then he asked her a second time. This time, lacking the will to refuse outright, she fled out of the room to take refuge in the nurses' lounge.

When she told her co-workers that she'd just turned him down a second time, the young nurses all looked at her in amazement, "You mean Ziemer on the fourth floor? That big hunk? Really? And you said 'No!' Are you nuts?" When my mother earnestly repeated the hospital rule against dating patients, her friend Sheila, a buxom redhead covered in freckles, told her, "If you're not interested in that gorgeous creature, one of us is! Next time you say 'Yes!' or else I'll ask to be put on his ward." So, my mother capitulated and said "Yes."

Some years later, when Mom asked Dad why he'd asked her to marry him, he said, "Well, Mary Jane turned me down." According to Mom, Mary Jane, Dad's high school sweetheart, was the one he "should have married". As it turned out, Mary Jane, who was a sportswoman, bossy as hell, and who could out curse Dad, didn't want to wait until he finished dental school to marry him. Instead, Dad ended up marrying Mom, who hated sports and hardly ever swore except when she stubbed her toe.

My parents married largely because my mother insisted that they do so before having sex. As Mom later explained it, during the months before the wedding, Dad managed to keep his hot temper under control, only losing it once on a date when he got mad and started cursing because they had to wait in line for tickets at the circus and then couldn't find their seats. Mom, who had been raised in a family of girls by mild-mannered parents, thought Dad was just showing off.

When the scantily clad, sequined assistant came out to hold the swing for the trapeze artist, Dad got a dopey grin on his face and his whole mood lifted. Recalling that evening and my dad's rage on the night, Mom would say incredulously, "To think I thought he was joking, Hah!"

On another date, they went to a restaurant in San Francisco's China Town. Mom's paper fortune slip read, "You will marry the person sitting across from you." At the time, she was smitten with the idea. Some forty years on, she remarked that if she'd known then what she knew later, she would have run out of the restaurant screaming. Although she was always quick to add that my brothers and I had made it all worth it, I didn't feel so sure about that.

As Mom later related, their first overnight trip should have been a warning. Dad had planned to take her to Yosemite National Park for a weekend trip in his 1939 Plymouth. All the way there, the Plymouth spewed noxious fumes and threatened to overheat. As they approached the entrance to Yosemite Valley, Dad suddenly said, "Let's go to Las Vegas. It's only a couple of hours away. While we're there we'll get married. I hate hassles, and it won't be a hassle to get married there." Mom thought, "Well, I'd like to see Las Vegas, but I'm certainly not getting married there." On the detour, the Plymouth broke down, putting an end to Dad's hassle-free wedding plans and sparing Mom and Dad a fight that might have ensured they'd never marry.

Dad pushed the car for half a mile, cursing all the way,

until he got it to where it could coast down the winding road to the park. By the time they rolled into the campground, it was dark, damp, and cold. Dad unknowingly laid their sleeping bags over a hill of ants. Just when he wanted to get romantic under the stars with Mom, she started to complain about the ants.

After finally moving to a new spot, Dad tried again with the kisses. This time, someone in the camp hollered, "A bear, a bear! Help, a bear!" Mom panicked and sat up stiff-backed. Dad lay on his back practically crying with frustration. Mom wouldn't lie down again until he got up to find out what was going on. As it turned out, someone going to the camp toilets in the night had found a bear drinking out of one of the toilet bowls. After the bear had lumbered off, Dad tried a third time to kiss Mom's neck. This time, she swatted him away and turned over in a huff. The rest of the night she shivered in her thin, damp sleeping bag. Spurned, Dad fell asleep, his snores reverberating in the canyon and Mom's ears.

The next night, Dad rented a "cabin". There was no running water and only a hot plate to cook on. Mom claimed she could still hear the bears sniffing around the campsite at night. Dad complained that Mom kept him up all night asking, "Walt, did you hear that? Walt!?"

The following day, as my future parents admired the Bridal Veil Falls, a plume of water tumbling over 600 feet into the valley, they ran into Dad's mother's best friend, Mary Ryder. Dad hadn't yet introduced Mom to his mother, so he felt awkward being "found out" on a weekend trip with a girl who wasn't even his fiancé. When he tried to make introductions, he was so nonplussed, he forgot Mom's name. Calmly, Mom extended her hand and said, "I'm Margaret. Pleased to meet you."

On the return trip to San Francisco, Dad pulled into a renowned grove of Giant Sequoias. At almost 300 feet in height, these pines are amongst the tallest and oldest trees in the world. He drove the old Plymouth through the Wawona Tunnel Tree, carved out of a massive Sequoia in 1881 to make way for wagons.[19] The Sequoias' towering beauty and spicy scent intoxicated Mom to the point where she forgave Dad for all that had gone wrong on their trip.

For once, Dad felt he'd done something right. He took hold of Mom's hand and pulled her towards a flower-strewn meadow. As they ran, Dad farted loudly. Mom, too polite to laugh outright, giggled silently, a sign of the inward, cryptic humor that would help her through the years to come. In the meadow, Dad took Mom in his arms and kissed her, and she at once forgot about the Plymouth, the curses, the ants, the bears, and the cold, sleepless nights.

My parents both look so young and beautiful in their wedding photographs. Friends of mine often admire the black and white shot Dad took of Mom in her wedding dress and ask if she was an actress. For his part, Dad looks like a movie star. Mom reported that at their wedding he sweated as hard as an actor under stage lights. After the ceremony, incensed by one of his friends who had kissed my mother ardently in the reception line, Dad refused to share the traditional slice of the wedding cake with Mom and walked out of the room cursing. He only returned because his best man grabbed him and said,

"Hey Ziemer, what's wrong with you?", pulling him back into the wedding reception.

Dad never wanted to be a father. Mom, on the other hand, who had trained as a pediatric nurse and who loved children, always planned on being a mother. As she tells it, she threatened to leave Dad if he didn't give her children. After all, she'd married him in part because he looked like good genetic stock, and, importantly, he was in dental school, so in future he would be able to support a family comfortably. Whenever Mom retold this, her jaw set just as it must have done when she made her threat.

On one hiking trip my dad confessed to me that he missed the attention he'd got from Mom before we kids came along. He lamented, "The wife gets a baby, and the hubby is second best. Another baby, and he's in third place. A third kid and he doesn't exist."

A few years after having my brothers, Mom lost a perfect baby boy still-born in the hospital and later another baby, miscarrying at home in the bathroom. As she sat sobbing on the toilet, Dad found her there. When he learned what had happened, he said, "What the hell are you crying about it for? I didn't want another boy anyway."

Despite her deep hurt then and over the years that followed, Mom still raved about Dad's appearance and would allude to the virility that evidently compensated for the dirty footprints he tracked down the hallway and the greasy fingerprints he left around the house after working in the garage. With a mixture of pride and repulsion, Mom told me that he insisted on making love to her when she once had a temperature of

105°F. She joked that she had relented because she was tired of him hanging around like a sad beast, but the truth was she feared that if he didn't get sex, he'd take his anger out on the family.

On weekends and some afternoons when Dad came home from the office for lunch, Mom would announce, "Dad and I are going to take a nap," or "Dad's crabby. It's time for a nap." That was the signal that my brothers and I were to keep quiet. My brothers even stopped their fighting. We knew that hour was sacrosanct and any interruptions on our part risked retribution.

Mom often took a bath before the nap, and I sensed that she was preparing herself for her time with Dad and that all their "naps" weren't really naps at all. Mystified, I'd hear the bed creaking rhythmically, too frightened to interrupt. By the time Mom got pregnant with me, she was thirty-eight. I was the result of an "accident" that occured during one of their naps.

Ironically, just at this time in her life, Mom had made up her mind to leave Dad. My birth sealed her fate. Mom bottled in her own frustration and resentful anger, turning it against herself. She became depressed, with a stubborn, passive resistance that strongly hinted at martyrdom.

During my childhood, I wordlessly absorbed her coping strategies to my own detriment, as reflected in the mirror imagery of the following dream, which I'll describe in three parts:

In this dream my former husband and I are on riding on a

roller coaster in an amusement park. The ride is set up like an old mine and we travel along a dark mineshaft. Feeling very tired, I doze off as we approach the exit and can't be roused. When I come to, I find myself alone in the car, in a passageway that has a large mirror mounted on the wall. My mother looks out at me from the mirror! She appears very much alive, and I call out to her, "Mummy, it's you. You're alive! You are so beautiful!" Although I am aware that she's died in waking life and that my use of the word "mummy" is unusual for me, I haven't yet realized I'm dreaming.

It then occurs to me that I should see my own reflection in the mirror, not my mother's. With this thought, my mother's face distorts, and she takes on a more frightening aspect. My mind races around trying to figure out what is going on, for this has never happened before. All this started with my beautiful mother. How can it be?

Finally, my mother becomes unrecognizable and monstrous with long nails. Thrusting her claw-like hands outside of the mirror's frame, she cuts the forefinger of my left hand with her nail, drawing blood. The sharp pain strikes me as unusual in a dream and with this perception, I become lucid and say calmly, "You have no power over me. This is a dream." Abruptly, the dreamscape then gives way to sparkling darkness.

Pointedly, my mother cut my left forefinger. Traditionally, the "left hand path" refers to the way of the soul and inner mysteries, while the forefinger points the way. Subsequently, I have understood this scene as the mirror revealing to me the anger that arises from frustrated instincts and desires, mine most surely but my mother's too, feelings that I had unknowingly absorbed over many years. Yet on another level, the reflection paradoxically may have mirrored my mother's growing frustration from "beyond the veil" with my continuing reluctance to face the "roller-coaster" of painful feelings about my marriage at the time.

I have found that when dream Beings or other creatures cut or bite the dreamer, they aim to draw attention. This may be a playful invitation, as was the nip the kid goat gave my fingers in the dream "Celestial Cities". However, when the dreamer ignores such invitations and neglects to integrate what they might mean into their waking life, then, as in this dream, the effect may literally be more "biting", as if to cut through the dreamer's defenses. In this way, I was being challenged to be more conscious of how I create my own reality and of what may be lacking or needed for change. Although getting bitten or cut in a dream may hurt, the action had positive implications for me, the pain of the cut snapping me out of my fear and waking me up to the realization that I had agency over the dream narrative.

I look back on this scene as portraying a painful truth about my lack of willpower at the time. The cut drew drops of blood — a clear call to move from the mind to the heart and to live more fully. I was made acutely aware that I had power over my fears, my choices in life, and could make changes.

This realization brought me to full lucidity, as the dream continued:

The winds take hold of me, and I begin to sing a song of praise and then cry out passionately, "Guide me!" After some time, my soul is taken into glittering darkness filled with crystals of light. As I pass by, each crystal emits music like wind chimes — musical scores of astounding beauty and depth. I regret that I lack the ability to repeat the melodies upon waking. It seems especially wondrous to me to hear such music because I don't think of myself as particularly musical.

Then it occurs to me that this may be the music of the celestial realms. The harmonious blend of sounds gives way to a trumpet playing a melody I know, the tune being one of my favorite hymns which I often sing before sleep: "You my God are my heart's desire and my soul cries out to Thee. You my God are my strength, my shield. To you oh Lord will your servant yield. You my God are my heart's desire and my soul cries out to Thee."

At the edge of the vast expanse where the crystals end, a diaphanous white veil moves in a gentle wind. A rich rose light radiates from behind the veil. I think to myself, "The Holy of Holies" and feel very humbled, wondering if I'll be allowed to approach any further.

The wind lifts the veil and I find myself in a dreambody, kneeling before a large object. The stone base has an inscription that begins with the name of Jesus. As soon as I try to read the rest, the script turns to hieroglyphics that I can't understand. Instead, I run my fingers over the letters, reading them like a blind person reading Braille. The knowing that enters through my fingertips fills my soul with the fullness of love, as if I were inside heartfelt tears. Looking up, I can see that upon the stone foundation there stands a Celtic cross of hammered gold about an inch in width. Backlit by the rose red light, the cross appears almost black.

My frustration and inaction, depicted at the start of the dream, found creative expression in the second half. The trumpet's call from within dream lucidity resonated with the purity of Divine desire, heralding the lifting of the veil, and drawing my heart further into revelation.

When the veil lifted, I was reminded of the Holy of Holies, the innermost place of the Hebrew Tabernacle, hidden by a veil. The veil's whiteness conveyed humble simplicity, and the rose light emanated love. The Celtic cross, in which a circle encompasses a symmetrical cross, symbolizes the union of matter and spirit, the place where human incompleteness is held by the wholeness of Divine love. It seemed fitting that the cross had Jesus's name inscribed on its stone base, for Jesus personifies the incarnation of Spirit.

What else was written on the base of the cross? In the dream, I intuited the meaning of the hieroglyphs through touch. As I now run my fingers over the computer keyboard to type this passage, the sensation returns, and it occurs to me that what was transmitted to me in the dream takes shape in my writing. The dream illustrates that there is more than one way to make music in the world!

Unexpectedly, the dream narrative then abruptly shifted to a new scenario:

I find myself still aware that I am dreaming and in a dream group led by one of my dream guides in waking life. At the front of the room stands a table with a dream machine on it. A member of the group sits at the table hooked up to the machine by cables that wrap around each of his fingertips and thumbs. This contraption apparently enables the dreamer to re-enter the dream with the dream guide. The guide works the controls and is thus able to be in the dream too. It appears that the dreamer is having a frightening experience like the one that I'd had earlier in the dream. He looks fearful and his body contorts with fear, so the dream guide calms him by saying, "Now you must tell them to go away. They have no power over you." Then I wake up.

Although I have retold this lucid dream sequentially, each part of the dream is nested within the others and within my life. Now, a decade later, I am heartened to see that it was through my struggles with my own limitations that I became lucid and thus open to the revelatory power of the dream vision and its implications for my waking life. Confronting my fear directly in the dream ultimately helped me to confront my fears in waking life and to take decisive action. This dream expanded my understanding of how Spirit is forged in the crucible of our lives.

The ending of this dream intimated that the learning from it would be integrated into my waking life and that my vocation would involve drawing on the Spirit's transformative power through dreams and dreamwork. In the coming years, I would go on to hold dream groups and, when working with a person frighted by a dream figure, have often repeated those words from the dream, "They have no power over you." When I feel afraid, this dream's central teaching reminds me of the biblical injunction "to be not afraid" [20] — in life or in dreams — for no fear exists in the love where Heaven and Earth touch.

Coming Home

Shortly after the loss of my mother, Dad told me they had wanted me to use my inheritance towards buying a property instead of renting, as my then husband and I had always done. A few years after my father passed, my parents' wish was finally fulfilled when we bought our own place in London.

The excitement of finding the new apartment and the effort of moving and settling in provided a distraction from long-standing marital difficulties. As many couples do, we fondly believed that owning a property and making a new home would provide us with a fresh start.

It was also important for me to live close by my work, where the counselling center had achieved charitable status and a measure of financial stability. The center's outreach had been widened by opening satellites in a nearby church and wellbeing clinic. These were busy, rewarding times, and moving into this little apartment, so near to my work, meant that I could walk there, regaining a sense of calm by praying or singing inwardly on my way.

Soon after the move, I had a lucid dream I called "The Greening", in which my mother made one of her rare appearances *within* dream lucidity. The dream begins in what appears to be the living room of the new place, but strangely altered:

Sitting in the living room, I notice that there is a circular hole, about two feet in diameter, in the center of the ceiling. Sunlight pours through the hole. Becoming angry about the defective roof, I wonder how we hadn't noticed that hole before. Yet, the column of light streaming in from the opening also reminds me of the axis mundi, the axis between the poles about which the Earth turns, and which, alchemically speaking, connects the physical and spiritual realms. I also notice that the room has been decorated in the same hot pink as my room at the age of five, but now with silver touches, "Can it really be silver?" I wonder.

From a mundane perspective, the hole in the ceiling was going to be a problem! Spiritually, however, it held great significance, for it marked an entry point for Spirit into the physical world. Although I made this connection in the dream, it only occurred to me later that it also symbolized the "crown chakra" of my subtle body, which in yogic practice signifies opening of the human mind and heart to the spiritual realms, while silver, too, is alchemically associated with the soul.

Upon waking, I felt puzzled as to why the room should be the same color as my bedroom from childhood. The answer came when I recalled my excitement when my mother let me choose my favorite color for my room, graciously agreeing to have it painted hot pink (also known as fuchsia), and which, in the dream, infused the new apartment with optimism and hope for the future.

Suddenly, the tone of the dream shifted abruptly:

A woman now enters whom I recognize as the punk rock

singer Courtney Love. She tells that me she has stolen some of the silver and is proud of it. I tell her she is a "bitch" for doing so and am so shocked at my having sworn that I become lucid.

This dream turned out to be so pivotal to my waking life that I need to expand on the meaning of this dream scene and its associations for me. Notorious for her sassy tone and "grungy" eroticism, Courtney Love was married to the musician Kurt Cobain, lead singer for the iconic band Nirvana. Both used heroin, and they had only been married for two tumultuous years when Cobain was persuaded to go into a drug rehabilitation center. After absconding, Cobain committed suicide, a tragic epitaph for Nirvana.

Shortly before the dream, I had watched a documentary about Love and Cobain's relationship in which it was implied, rightly or wrongly, that Courtney's behavior and threats to end the marriage pushed Cobain to suicide. Like Love and Cobain, my husband and I, despite our gifts, were hooked into repeating our own scenarios of conflict, each time expecting things to be different. I had begun to see that our relationship would need to end if either one of us was to grow further but feared my husband would harm himself and that the process would be damaging for me too.

Courtney's presence brought out not only my fears about divorce but also challenged the unhelpful idealizations I had held about marriage. Calling her a "bitch" for stealing the silver from the room, broke the spell, if only momentarily. It also meant I would have to face and name the ways that I had been robbing myself of my soul by staying in a situation that was, in fact, bad for both my husband and me. The dream foreshadows the "bitchy" determinedness I would need to find in myself to get through the divorce process.

The word "bitch" in the dream is laden with a childhood memory that only now comes to mind. When I was four, a friend of mine a few years older than me, got me to knock on the door of an elderly woman living on our street and to call out, "Bitch!", which I did matter-of-factly, not knowing what the word meant.

When we returned to my family home, with great pride, I promptly told my mother what I had just done. In front of my friend, she spanked me for the first and only time in my life! Feeling confused, I ran into my bedroom and cried. Years later, my mother admitted that she too thought this woman was "bitchy" and that she regretted her actions.

After that, I almost never used this swear word again. The experience left me feeling that it wasn't acceptable to name bad behavior even when it was called for. However, my shock at myself in the dream for using such a swear word had the effect of initiating lucidity, the dream imagery immediately dissolving into bright darkness:

> *The soft blackness on which I am carried washes through my soul like grace. An emerald light arises from the palm of my hands, illuminating my fingers like vibrant leaves.*
>
> *The hole in the ceiling transforms into the entrance of a "wormhole", reverberating with geometric, crystalline patterns of the same vibrant light. "Oh, the green!" I think, "This is*

the Spirit! This is the 'greening'!", which fills me with hope.

After being pulled through the wormhole, I emerge on the other side with a dreambody to find myself in a great house, lined with wood paneling and beautiful peacock-colored wall coverings in a design by William Morris, the 19th century English artist. My mother, her blond hair shining, stands in the room as if she has been waiting for me.

She shows me around, but my mind becomes confused because the dream feels so real. Along with my confusion, a sense of claustrophobia arises, waking me and leaving me feeling sad to have missed the rest of what my mother was so keen to share with me.

Unlike most of my lucid dreams, this one felt "unfinished", its intent unclear. This was the first time in many years that my mother had met me in her full bodily form within dream lucidity, looking much as she had in waking life, only more vibrant.

In previous lucid dreams, my mother had usually appeared at the threshold of a new dimension, one which I would then enter on my own, carrying the memory of her presence as reassurance. Here, however, meeting her on the "other side" of the wormhole, it felt as if I had been brought to visit her in her new home, a place where the fullness of her soul could shine. Exuding self-possession and joy, she gave me a taste of what a true homecoming can feel like.

The wall coverings by William Morris reminded me my mother's love for his style and the artistic movement his work inspired. Yet, apart from her early attempt to decorate the family living room with a peacock-colored marble table and a sofa covered in a floral weave, she never again brought such design elements into our family home. It seems even stranger to me now that she did not do any artwork herself, although she often showed me a sketch book from her youth filled with her lovely illustrations, recalling how she and her two sisters would spend hours drawing as children. I can't help but wonder why she denied herself the pleasure of artistic creation. Perhaps she never felt at home where we lived, nor within herself, feelings with which I have also struggled.

Very likely the humble elegance and gentle beauty of Morris' designs seemed out of place to her in the hard-edged suburban environment in which we lived. Inwardly, she had closed the door on her own gifts, considering instead her children to be her life's work. I would like to think that for both of us the room's capacious beauty, its rich peacock-colors and handmade furniture, skillfully and lovingly carved, stood as a promise of an inner potentiality awaiting full realization in the physical world.

Upon waking, I couldn't help but notice that the house of my dream, with its stately yet inviting living space, contrasted starkly with the actuality of my cramped apartment. Yet, by means of a wormhole, I had been transported to a new, spacious dimension. Indeed, after this dream, many unusually powerful wormholes began to appear in my lucid dreams, a phenomenon I detail in my book *Lucid Surrender*. [21]

Not long after this dream, my monthly periods stopped altogether. The finality of this compelled me to accept that the marriage would be childless, and my hope for us as a couple finally died. The visceral realization was conclusive and led to our divorce.

In time, I would move from the urban environment of London to the English countryside. My new home there would have many touches of Arts and Crafts design, including some of William Morris' endearing patterns, reflecting my yearning to write, live and love with simplicity and grace.

The "greening" to which I referred in this dream connects with this desire. It alludes to an expression coined by the mystic, writer and musician, Hildegard of Bingen, a Benedictine Abbess of the twelfth-century, who used the Latin term *viriditas* to express the regenerative "Divine Force of God in Nature". [22]

The "greening" of my world would grow not only through my work with dreams but also in the flourishing of my eventual new marriage. My mother beckoned me on to find fulfilment in life here on Earth. I am so glad to know she is giving expression to her soul's beauty in the world beyond.

Part Four
Lessons in Life and Beyond

The Eternal Well of Living Light

Consoled as I was by my mother's presence in my dreams, navigating divorce and the demands of work had exhausted me, and it felt hard to face yet another spring weighed down by responsibilities and the grind of city life. My dreams had seemingly dried up too. For a time, I felt out of touch with Spirit's guidance; far from a sacred quality within myself. I thirsted for the Spirit's living waters. [23]

One night, unable to pray, feeling lonely and unsure of my next move, I wondered, "How has this happened? How can I set it right? How can I best serve in a more soulful way?" In quiet desperation, I called out to the Holy Spirit for guidance.

Then an old familiar hymn came to me, "He shall feed his flock like a shepherd. He shall gather the lambs in his arms and carry them in his bosom and shall gently lead those that are with young."[24] I clearly heard my mother's voice carrying the tune, and the innocent beauty of her singing made me tearful.

Such tender, loving grace had felt far from me and my surroundings. For some time, I'd had to be "tough" personally and professionally. The song softened my heart, especially as this was the first (and only) time my mother had made her presence known to me before I entered the dream state.

Curled up in bed, with my eyes partially closed, I began to feel the lucid space open within me. A voice behind me said, "Turn to me" so I turned over onto my back in response. As I exhaled through my mouth, my soul moved out of my body and onto the Black Light through the opening between my lips — a novelty for me! My soul then plunged downwards, reminding me of Alice in Wonderland's precipitous fall down the rabbit hole: [25]

> *As my soul descends into the dark light, familiar feelings of despondency and loneliness plague me, until I recall that I am not alone and call out to the angels: "Are you angels there?" In response, two Beings of swirling red light appear in the glowing blackness before me to my right and to my left, twisting and turning gracefully. They continuously bow in adoration and then rise in praise to God as they accompany me on the descent, spiraling downwards. Seeing them so absorbed in their worship amazes and comforts me. Their beauteous, fluid light calls to my soul, beckoning me on.*

By the time of this lucid dream, I had learned from experience that angels of light fill the apparent emptiness of the lucid void. It seems to me they mostly remain invisible to help us gain the faith we need to move forward into our soul's longing. When revealed, they appear to our eyes in accordance with our capacity to see and in response to our need.

Viewed through the eye of the heart, they have revealed themselves to me as pure Beings of Light. Other times, depending on the heart's openness, they have taken on the form of a wise person or animal, or even as encouraging signs, an eagle feather or a shiny stone that catches the eye, a word of guidance from an open book, a candle's glow — signifiers of grace. I understand all such signs to be love tokens from those celestial Beings, giving form and action to God's love.[26] Sufis say that an angel goes out before each one of us to lead us into becoming the Spirit's light in the world:

> *Now the angels guide me to the center point of the illuminated darkness where there appears a black hollow cylinder several feet across in diameter that looks rather like the opening of a well. Having been set down next to it, I can see that an infinite, gleaming expanse, full of star-like pinpricks of light, fills the well. Immediately, I exclaim, "The Divine!"*
>
> *I stand up and, bending down, place my hands on either side of the opening and peer into its mysterious beauty. Without warning, I am pulled headfirst into it, my dream-body dissolving into the star-laced blackness. Wondrous filaments of white light now move through my soul. "Oh, fill me!" I cry out, feeling cleansed, immensely grateful, and relieved.*

This experience brought home to me that just as Nature's life force, enriched by water and light, takes root in the darkness, so too, in Lucid Surrender, Beings and forms of light blossom from the depths of Black Light.

In this well's dark illumination, my soul received filling and renewal from what I later called, "The Eternal Well of Living Light" — the wellspring of God's unbounded Being:

> *After I spend some time suspended in the well's beauty, I find myself lifted out of it and once again set down next to*

it. From this vantage point, I can see that the edges of the well's cylinder are spinning to the left, and from this spinning, silvery star-like Beings materialize.

Kneeling again before the edge and placing my hands on either side of the rim to aid the turning, the thought comes, "Sweet silver angels!" My hands feel alive with energy as the spinning creates a music to which the angels sing. I begin to sing along with them, filled with joy. Eventually, the vision ends, and I rouse myself, wishing I could recall the music and share it in waking life.

Reflecting on this revelation, the star-lined well makes me think of a cosmological "black hole", except that here was not so much a nursery for stars as for angels, celestial Beings of Light, messengers of God's might and mercy, will and love.

How wonderful to take part in the birth of these radiant Beings! Having opened myself to the Highest Will in Lucid Surrender, the eye-of-my-heart could see the splendor of angels singing Creation into Being and encircling humanity in Love's song, much as my mother's tender singing had initiated the vision and encompassed me in love.

The Refining Fire of Spirit

Through the ages, mystics have told of a strange fire whose flames can burn hot or cold. Ultimately, this fire, alive with Spirit and ignited by Love, refines and renews the heart. The more inwardly divided a person may be, the more this subtle fire burns with increasing heat and intensity. Paradoxically, the more a person has a singleness of purpose aligned with the innermost desire of the heart, the cooler this fire burns.

From the alchemical perspective, fire in a dream generally signifies purification and change. Destruction by an intensely hot fire may mirror or portend chaotic, self-destructive actions on the dreamer's part in waking life or a sudden dramatic shift in life circumstances. However, a fire that does not consume what it burns, like the burning bush from which the Hebrew God, Yahweh, speaks to Moses,[27] points to a readiness in the dreamer to follow a new life path, even when the dreamer doesn't feel up to the task. In all cases, fire transforms, putting the dreamer in touch with qualities essential to their nature that are needed to complete the spiritual work that lies ahead.

As an illustration of this spiritual fire in my own dreams, I'll return to a dream of mine that I had shortly after the legalities of my divorce were finally completed, leaving me free to look to the future. A key image in this dream was my doll, Honeybunch, who once belonged to my mother:

I dream that I own an open-plan, two-story log cabin. One of my brothers has come for a visit. He suddenly tells me that the house in on fire, so we must get out, but that I have time to get a couple of things. I feel sad, but also glad to think, "Well, I can start over again." The only "thing" that I want to take is Honeybunch. My brother and I are on the second floor, where we can see the flames lapping up from floor to ceiling, but we do not feel their heat. I begin to worry about how we will get out if the stairs are on fire. Will we have to jump? Then I awake.

This dream, "Transforming Fire", also appears in my book *The Hidden Lives of Dreams*. Here, I want to say more about my experience of spiritual fire and how this fire relates to Honeybunch and to the women in my family.

Only on reflection many years later did it occur to me that the fire in this dream gave off no heat, nor did it burn me. Yet, in the dream, unable to surmount my instinctual reaction, I did not comprehend the fire's spiritual import and missed the chance to become lucid. Nonetheless, in the dream, the fire's presence instilled within me the realization that there was enough spirit in me to "start over again".[28]

In time, I also came to understand more fully what Honeybunch represented. Explaining this means going back to Honeybunch's "birth" in 1936. As told to me by my mother, 1936 was the year that my grandpa went off to the Yukon in Alaska in search of gold during the Great Depression. Grandpa was a Welsh Williams and Grandma, a Scotch-Irish McCray. Both could sing like birds and wrote songs and poetry. He and Grandma had met in the Methodist church choir in Seattle, Washington. Grandpa later said he had to marry Grandma because he had kissed her once after choir practice! Not long after their marriage, he stood up at the end of choir practice, said he couldn't believe in the church anymore and walked out, never to return. After that, as my mother told it, he never could hold down a job.

When Grandpa left for Alaska that spring, neither he nor Grandma knew she was pregnant for the fourth time. One winter's night, my mom, then aged nine, heard thumps coming from her mother's room. She peeked in the room and watched silently as her mother rolled off her high bed to the floor repeatedly, crying softly. Only later as an adult did Mom realize that Grandma was trying to abort the pregnancy.

To support the family, Grandma had taken a job as a substitute teacher, leaving home early, often on rainy mornings, to travel by bus to work. As Christmas approached, she finally received a letter from Grandpa in Alaska. She was hoping for news of a gold strike. In anticipation, she waited until the evening to open the letter. She washed and towel-dried her long hair, made herself a cup of tea, sliced off a piece of the Milky Way bar that she kept hidden as a rare treat in her medicine chest, and then gathered her three daughters around her before opening the letter. Instead of money, she found a large piece of skin peeled from Grandpa's face after it had been badly burnt by the sun reflected off the Alaskan snows, along with the flattened body of a large mosquito that he'd also enclosed to prove its enormity.

In a fit of rage, Grandma ran down into the basement and

hurled all Grandpa's love letters, along with her poetry and the songs she had written, into the furnace. As the fire burned, my mother and her two sisters, who had raced down the stairs after Grandma, watched in horror as she cut off her long curls and cursed the day that she'd married Grandpa. Not long after that, she miscarried a baby boy.

The next day, Grandma gathered up her hair, took it to the local wigmaker's shop and sold most of it for a goodly sum, using this money to buy each of her three daughters the same kind of doll for Christmas. She then had the wigmaker use the rest of the hair to make a wig for each doll. While the dolls were being prepared, Grandma spent many hours in secret, sewing a fine set of dresses, coats, and hats for each doll. (Whereas my aunts kept their dolls wardrobes intact, by the time my mother passed Honeybunch on to me, she only possessed the one dress — a rather tattered blue and white pinafore.)

As a child, I would brush Honeybunch's ringlets, unaware of my grandma's rage and how she turned it against herself. Now when fingering her curls, I sense that the strands must have held a profound sorrow and an almost suicidal fury, for when Grandmother cut off her hair, she was symbolically destroying a cherished and feminine part of herself.

In Honeybunch, she may have found a way to make a gift of her anger, but she also passed on a harmful dynamic of self-abnegation that my mother mirrored in her own life and which, in turn, had undermined my sense of agency so that I could not assert my yearning for children of my own.

When my mother told me the story of Grandpa's trip to the Yukon, she made it sound as if it had all been an adventure for him. At the end the story, she mused aloud, "Poor man, he could never get anything right." But I also see the story as poignant, a man going North to Alaska with great hopes of striking it rich, only to have his dreams dashed against the harsh reality of the Alaskan climate. Possibly the contents of his letter were meant to express the extent of his own inner torment and desperation. Yet, he and Grandma could not find a way to communicate their respective needs, nor to share in alleviating them.

After my mother died, I found some letters, yellowed with age, that she'd sent to Grandpa while he was in Alaska. In one she had written, "Grandma Williams' birthday was yesterday. She was seventy-five years old. Hope you come home before you are that old," and in another, "Everybody is lonesome for you, especially your wife and children". Still a child at the time, my mother, who so dearly missed Grandpa's fun-loving presence, gave voice to a precocious sensibility in which her parents were not able to share.

The making of Honeybunch is a story of conflicting emotions. On the one hand, there simmers the pain of frustration and sacrifice of the creative feminine. On the other, Honeybunch symbolizes my mother's enduring love for me and the love of all the women who came before us and who have struggled to relate forthrightly to themselves and others, not least their husbands. The dream gave me confidence in the future because it felt to me that through Honeybunch, my mother, Grandma, and all the women in our family line stood behind me, willing me to move forward into life and to have the courage to realize my dreams.

When I shared the story of Honeybunch with a colleague, herself a gifted artist and seamstress who had once owned a dress shop featuring her designs, she kindly offered to sew a new outfit for Honeybunch. In the end, she made two, a fine cotton and linen dress for summer and a red velvet gown for winter, both with petticoats, caps, and capes. The dresses suited Honeybunch well, bestowing a rich and hard-won beauty upon her. Her new wardrobe perfectly expressed my soul's desire to be outfitted anew.

Living Waters

Two years after my divorce, I found myself preparing to leave my job at the counselling center where I had worked for nearly ten years, first as a volunteer counsellor, then as manager, and finally, director. Would my next move be a return to the United States or moving into a new way of life in the United Kingdom? My soul longed to know the blessings of creative fruition alongside finding a mature love. In the months prior to the dream of "Celestial Tigers" featured in this chapter, I had been dating Andrew, a wonderful man whom I would go on to marry the following spring.

That night in my prayers, I asked for confirmation that I was on the right path, and the lucid dream, which followed in three sections, confirmed my choices through a powerful sequence of scenes. In the first of these, magnificent tigers in groups of three or four circled atop onyx-black boulders. They moved with such fluidity and speed that they looked like flames swirling with a fierce yet focused intensity:

> *As I look on, more tigers materialize against the backdrop of vibrant darkness. For a moment, I feel afraid that they might leap down and devour me. Recalling the biblical story of "Daniel in the Lion's Den", I know that the tigers could easily overpower me if they chose to, so I decide to stay calm. The tigers remain centered on their circling, communicat-*

ing a steady willpower and creative energy. I begin to sense that these tigers represent celestial Beings that have revealed themselves to me.

I wonder what the tigers will do and if they will speak or silently share with me their awesome beauty and concentrated power. Then the lucid dream comes to a sudden close, as a knight-like Being swoops me up and carries me back across the Black Light. How I would have liked to spend more time with the magnificent creatures!

In my book, *Lucid Surrender*, I conclude the account of this dream at this point. However, the unabridged lucid dream continued with the emergence of a second dreamscape:

I am deposited in a house where I wait for Andrew to pick me up to go out. The house looks vaguely familiar. I think of my parents and recall that they have died in waking life. Andrew enters. Then my former husband comes out of a room looking angry at seeing us together. He begins to challenge Andrew rudely, but I come between them and tell him to stop, saying calmly and assertively "It's done now. You have no right. I understand you are upset but you can't do this."

Unexpectedly, a little fairy-like girl, who has appeared in other dreams of mine, enters, takes hold of my ex-husband's hand, and pulls him away as if to say, "Time to go now, come with me!" She has come to my aid before in similar dreams, and I feel grateful.

At the same time, I also want to express gratitude to my former husband for the good that we once shared and gave to each other. He turns towards me, and I say these things across the space separating us. Then the fairy tugs him along, leaving me feeling relieved and with a sense of closure.

The message held in this part of the dream seems straight forward enough, but I will add here that the energy of the tigers had given me the willpower needed to face the personal challenge of the confrontation that followed. My awareness that my parents had both died years before signified to me in the dream that their story no longer overruled my own.

The dream then concluded:

Turning to meet Andrew, I suddenly find myself wearing the white blouse and black skirt I often wear when sitting with him on warm days in his garden. Now, however, I am walking by a pool filled with glistening aqua-marine water. Suddenly, I tumble in! The water pushes up my blouse and skirt like a balloon, which helps me to float.

To my surprise, my mother is sitting at the edge of the pool with her feet in the water. I realize she has appeared in her subtle body since I know that she has died. Smiling, she watches me swim on my back with my belly exposed. When I tighten my belly, water squirts from my navel like a fountain and falls around in sparkles of green light. My mother "oohs" and "aahs" with pleasure at this. As I begin to tire, I wake up feeling weary, yet glad to feel confirmed in my life choices.

The scene of my mother at the pool's edge parallels a similar scene in waking life at my brother Carey's home in North Carolina, shortly after we had taken my mother there to live out her final days in accordance with her wishes. In those first weeks at Carey's, when Mom still had some strength, she liked to sit on the sofa in the family room overlooking the pool in the backyard and watch me swimming.

Through the sliding glass door, she would smile wanly at me as she raised her arm, waving wistfully as if she were already viewing me from a different dimension. These tender gestures of love and longing made my heart ache. The pool's water hid my tears.

To fly Mom from California to North Carolina, a close friend of Carey's, who had loved our mom as if she were his own, donated air miles so that she, my brother, Steve, and I could fly first class. Although too unwell to enjoy all the amenities of five-star travel, Mom nevertheless relished the chance to fly in style for her final flight.

Mom's trip to North Carolina took me back to memories of our first airline trip together, when she was forty-three and I was five. We dressed up to fly from Los Angeles to her hometown of Seattle. Mom wore a pale-yellow white skirt with white trim and a matching cardigan, smart pale-yellow shoes, white gloves, and a little yellow hat.

At the time, flying was still a novelty for most people, and pricey, too. Mom had saved up for our tickets, and it felt like a special occasion. The staff served free champagne and smiled attentively. Passengers craned excitedly from their spacious seats to look out of the windows at the stunning view below. The future seemed to unfurl before our eyes as my mother and I flew over the dramatic landscapes of the Western United States.

Our last flight together felt very different, more like a sacred pilgrimage. The landmarks beneath us — the wide sheaths of the Mojave Desert and the high peaks of the Sierra Nevada mountains — took on the aura of revered sites, evoking memories of our family's adventures (and misadventures) on Dad's camping trips. As we mused on the past and dealt with her present needs, neither of us could have dreamed of our future flights together in the subtle realms.

Taken together, the three parts of the lucid dream formed a triptych of inner being: the first expressed through the tigers the natural intelligence and might of the Spirit; the second mirrored the development of my personal psychology; and the third, symbolized the joy that, in the words of the old Sunday School song, can bubble up "like a fountain" in the soul, even in the midst of confusion and weariness.

My mother's presence by the poolside at the dream's end felt deeply affirming, for she took pleasure in watching me "in the swim of things", knowing that the living waters of the subtle realm both supported and moved through me as I entered a new chapter of my life.

The Healing Power of Lucidity

My mother's presence by the poolside at the end of the dream "Celestial Tigers", fifteen years after her death, was the last time she would appear in bodily form in a lucid dream of mine for some time. Looking back on the dream now, I see that my waking life and the dream world had come full circle in their mirroring. When nearing the end of her life, my mother had lovingly waved farewell as she watched me swimming for the last time. Similarly, in "Celestial Tigers", she bid me a wordless farewell from beyond, her work in the subtle realms on my behalf seemingly completed.

Since that dream, my mother's presence in my dreams has primarily been revealed through possessions of hers, such as her pearl necklace, her doll Honeybunch, or through words that evoke memories of her. One such dream, which I have called "My Mother's Sadness", occurred just over a month after "Celestial Tigers" and takes its name from words spoken by an unknown woman within the lucid dream. These words voiced my mother's earthly struggle for self-realization, a legacy she passed to me. "My Mother's Sadness" marks a watershed in the lucid dreams that had come to me since her death.

This dream took place during my final weeks as director of the counselling center. The day before, the familiar feeling of pushing myself too hard had taken hold of me. Before going to sleep, I asked myself why this should be so. The dream came in response, which I share here in two parts:

> *The dream begins in a modern church painted silvery blue. Three wide wings of pews fan out symmetrically from the pulpit at the center. A lively congregation fills the pews. My colleague Nigel Hamilton and I are there to give talks about lucid dreaming. The minister introduces us with enthusiasm, sharing a video about the Dream Research Institute that Nigel and I co-founded and how it provides a place for people to study and research dreams and wellbeing.*
>
> *In celebration of this, people in the congregation stand up and unfurl large bolts of silk cloth in bright, solid colors, throwing the rolls up in the air where they adhere to the ceiling and hang down like curtains. Some of the rolls fall back down and are tossed up again joyfully. I worry someone might get hurt, but so far, everyone seems fine. The banners remind me of beautiful temple veils.*
>
> *Then the host, a woman dressed glamorously in silver sequins goes to the pulpit and talks about Creative Imagination and the Imaginal realm. She, too, throws a bolt of colored cloth up towards the ceiling. The atmosphere feels celebratory and one of praise. My turn to speak approaches, so I go to find a restroom where I can change into more formal clothes and freshen up.*

This first part of the dream clearly mirrored my joy at having found a context in which to speak about dreams and to introduce others to the spiritual nature of lucid dreaming. Yet, on recollecting this dream, there was a sense of intoxication in the atmosphere that made me uneasy.

This dreamscape emerged out of my experience of sharing what I had learned in lucidity. For five years, I had been following my own dream guidance to share my lucid dreams, finding an inspirational platform through the International Association for the Study of Dreams.[29] As a member, I spoke at conferences and wrote magazine articles and book chapters for publication, also serving on the Board and as Vice President.

During this time, Nigel and I launched the Dream Research Institute (DRI) at the Centre for Counselling and Psychotherapy Education in London. Initially, I did my DRI dreamwork on the weekends and in the early hours of the morning while working fulltime, but I soon realized that I would wear myself out doing so. Over the next few years, I cut back my hours at the counselling center while transitioning to a primary focus on dreams and dream lucidity.

The imagery of colored banners suggested to me that sharing my dreams and dreamwork was my soul's way of bringing the colors of the creative mind into the world — each color an expression of light and of the qualities the color holds. Yet, as the dream indicated, I did not feel fully comfortable with the showier aspect of such celebrations or with wearing my soul on my sleeve, so to speak. Feeling distinctly underdressed for the occasion, I needed to look for a place where I could prepare myself:

> *I leave by the church's back gate and find myself in a much less beautiful alleyway that opens onto an urban environment. When I return to the church, a guard stands at the*

door trying to deal with a young woman who has apparently taken an overdose. I go over to help them and comfort her. "What have you injected?" I ask. She replies, "My mother's sadness". It's clear to me that although her reply seems strange, the injection is nonetheless very real and potentially deadly, like an actual narcotic. Her words remind me of how I have carried my mother's sadness throughout my own waking life.

As the young woman drifts into unconsciousness, I hold her and tell her she must stay awake, or she will die. Holding her like a baby, I rock her gently in my arms talking to her sweetly until she passes the crisis point. When she recovers, I realize that I'm late for my talk but feel unconcerned. I ask the young woman whether she will give me permission to share what just happened, and she says, "Yes."

We enter the main church, and the host leads me up to the pulpit. I tell the audience that I have appreciated the beauty of their service and the way they praise Jesus with such enthusiasm and joy, adding that if they want to know about the true nature of lucid dreaming, then I will tell them about what had just taken place outside. I do this and go on to say that when we know what matters most, when we stop long enough to be attentive and act with compassion and surrender "to what is", then we discover real lucidity. It's not quite what the audience expected from me.

After the talk, a man questions whether it was appropriate to tell the girl's story while she was present. I say, "I want to demonstrate how, when we step out of our set plans, new things open up. The girl understands this."

The host comes out and invites me to lunch. I wonder if

she'll be upset with me for delivering a different talk to the one planned, but she seems happy, which reassures me. Then, I awake.

By the time of this dream, both the counselling center and I had gained our independence. Growing in freedom to act in the outer world had come together with release from the lifelong effect of my mother's sadness. I could now understand that the young woman, who in my dream had overdosed on her mother's sadness, was both a part of my mother and of me.

In caring for the young woman with compassion and gently shepherding her to full consciousness, I found healing for the girl, for myself, and for my mother. At the same time, for such is the power of lucidity, my mother, through the dreams, had been helping me discover how to live life with joy!

Wearing Soul on the Outside

Two years after my release from my mother's sadness, Andrew and I were about to celebrate our first wedding anniversary. By now, the two of us had settled into our new life together in rural England.

Alongside my work at the Dream Research Institute, I continued to see clients and, for a year, served as the Vice President to the International Association for the Study of Dreams. During this time, Andrew published two volumes of his own therapeutic work, [30] material we took pleasure in reviewing together — just as we later enjoyed revising my books on dreams.

My own writing continued in the form of book chapters and magazine articles, but I had yet to write a book on dreams and dream lucidity. Would I ever pull together all my many hundreds of dreams into a coherent reflection of what they had taught me? Numerous dreams Beings were telling me to "finish the book" but the writing eluded me. My time and energy felt too dispersed, and while my lucid dreams had remained intense, simply recording them, left little time for writing anything else.

The following dream, which I have called "Wearing Soul on the Outside", removed my doubts, and spurred me to put pen to paper. The dream's opening scene reflected a day that had been filled with challenging emotions:

Looking at myself in my bedroom mirror, I see that my right eye has nearly swollen shut, looking as if I've been in a fight. Realizing that the mirror reflects an internal state from the day's emotions, I become lucid.

Immediately, the iridescent black winds carry me towards what looks like the eye of a hurricane but which, from other lucid dreams, I know is a wormhole. The wormhole draws my soul into an incredibly powerful and ecstatic descent so that maintaining a sacred focus is difficult. At the wormhole's end, I find myself set down in a space lit up like moonlight. A man stands next to me. I don't know who he is, but sense that he has brought me here and I am comforted by his calm, intelligent presence.

A woman then approaches holding a delicate crown that reminds me of my mother's wedding tiara. Diamond-like, moon-drop jewels drape over her fingers. She says, "These jewels are the birthright of your soul, taken from you but kept safely, and now restored for you to wear as you start over in your life." It is made clear to me that the lucid dreams will be abating, and that it is now the time to start wearing these jewels of my soul on the outside.

The woman moves to put the tiara on my head. Her gravitas and grace, the beauty and feeling of the jewels, touches me deeply. They have the quality of the light from both the sun and the moon.

Suddenly, I feel tremendously sad to have been missing out on this treasure trove of inner wealth, and yet both humbled and grateful to be given the chance to share with others what I have learned "before it's too late" — as the *dreams have been telling me. Grief that I was not able to access these jewels earlier in my life overwhelms me, and I begin to weep. As I kneel in reverence at the woman's feet, my tears awaken me.*

"Wearing my soul on the outside" meant writing and speaking about dreams. My passion for dreams could now wed with my love for writing. As for my mother's wedding tiara that appears in the dream, this had once clasped her wedding veil, and for all these years, I have kept safe the tiara of faux diamonds. It still sparkles with the promise it once held for my mother when she chose it, full of great hopes for a home and happiness.

Not long after this dream, I was commissioned to write a book on dreams and wellbeing, resulting in the publication of *The Hidden Lives of Dreams*, closely followed by *Lucid Surrender: The Alchemy of the Soul in Lucid Dreaming*. [31]

A month before the publication of *Lucid Surrender*, I had a dream that reassured me of my mother's contentment, even though I had been unable to fulfil her hope that I might have children:

Entering my parents' bedroom, I see my brother, Carey, and his wife resting on one side of the bed watching the television, and, on the other, my mother, who I know died many years before. Next to her on the floor, my two nieces sit, happily playing with their babies.

My mother wears her familiar pink, chiffon nightdress, looking joyful to be surrounded by her son and daughter-

in-law, grand-children, and great-grandchildren. I realize they can't see her lying there looking up at the ceiling, her arms extended by her sides, with her palms open.

I cry out, "Mother, you've come back!" Everyone asks me what I can see, but I remain silent as I don't want to lose my connection with her. She looks so alive, just as she did in waking life. Leaning over the bed, I stroke her forehead with my hand, telling her over and over, "I love you so much!"

All too soon, her skin, which looks so vital, begins to turn an alabaster white. I think of it as light, and know she will be going back from whence she came. She looks straight up at the ceiling the entire time smiling contentedly. I begin to cry and with my tears, wake up, feeling hopeful.

This dream, which I have entitled, "Motherly Love", gave me solace because it seemed that my mother's earthly desire had been made complete, knowing that my brothers and their families would carry on the family line.

Since having the dream "Motherly Love", the completion of this third book has brought about a healing of another kind to me and to my mother in spirit. As a child, I had held my mother's wedding tiara in my hands, full of wonder at its beauty, happily unaware that it, too, was only costume jewelry. In my teens and as a young adult, I felt angry my mother didn't have the real diamonds she deserved. Later, I came to appreciate that my mother and father were simply two human beings, who, despite their shortcomings, had done their best to live and love, while raising a family.

Yet, the story doesn't end there, for my lucid dreams with

my mother suggest to me that we can grow in wisdom and love beyond the grave and that emotional healing on one side of the veil brings healing to the other. And so, my mother's tiara of old came to be transformed into the priceless light of the soul.

List of Dreams

Prologue
The Letter from Beyond the Veil

Part One
The Blue Room
The Silver Cord
Soul Space
The Dress
My Mother's Death
The Ka'ba
Night Sky
Entering the Mirror
The Blue Mosque
On the Breath
The Blue Guitar

Part Two
The Fingerprint of God
Ensoulment
Body of Light
The Emerald City

Part Three
Come Home
Gifts of the Spirit
The Open Window
Black Lace Light
Black Lace Light II
The Celtic Cross
The Greening

Part Four
Eternal Well of Living light
Transforming Fire
Celestial Tigers, Unabridged
My Mother's Sadness
Wearing Soul on the Outside
Motherly Love

Treasured Family Memories

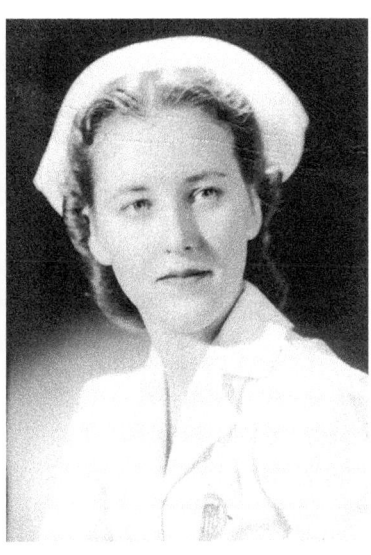

Margaret before meeting Walt

Young love

Margaret full of joy and hope

The handsome Walt

The Wawona Tunnel Tree date

Mr and Mrs Ziemer

The Ziemer family home

My brothers Steve and Carey and me

Travels in the jeep

Margaret's last outing – still finding a smile

NOTES

1. This dream also appears in my book *Lucid Surrender: The Alchemy of the Soul in Lucid Dreaming* (Dorset, England: Archive Publishing) 38-40. However, I highlight different aspects of the dream in this treatment.
2. Chapter Nine of *Lucid Surrender*, "Through the Looking Glass in Lucidity", looks at nine lucid dreams that I had over a twenty-year period involving mirrors, their reflections pointing to a deep knowledge both of oneself and of the Divine.
3. The Blue Mosque's official name is Sultan Ahmed Mosque. It was completed in 1616.
4. 1 Corinthians 3:16 (Berean Literal Bible).
5. Acts 17:24 (New International Version).
6. The International Association of Dreams provides a forum for those interested in dreamwork and research. I have been grateful for the organization's support over the years.
    See https://www.asdreams.org
7. To make space for the mall, an entire orange grove was cut down, a harbinger of the unbridled development that would consume Southern California's ranchlands and farms. The mall marked the onslaught of "consumer culture" that overtook the area as more shopping malls, restaurants and grocery stores went up. It also reminds me of the unhappy shopping trips my mother and I took there in my teen years to buy clothes that would help me "fit in" at school, though rather unsuccessfully. Before the mall was built, clothes didn't matter so much at school. Afterwards, clothing became an indicator of "status". By the time I was in my twenties, massive warehouse-style stores had been built, requiring yet more land to be covered in concrete. I naively thought Europe would be different. It was for the first few years I lived there, but then all the brands from the US moved in, crowding out the local economy and natural landscape.
8. The Ark is said to have held three items: a gold jar of manna, the unleavened bread that God provided the Israelites with during their forty years of wandering in the desert; the staff of Moses' brother Aaron, which budded with blossoms and almonds as proof that Aaron was meant to be the first priest of Israel; and the stone tablets bearing

the ten commandments that God gave to Moses. The inner "Holy of Holies" contains spiritual nourishment, gives evidence of and confidence in the Spirit's gifts and testifies to the law of love that is written on the heart.

9. The idea that a person could be killed for approaching the Holy of Holies with an impure heart is derived from the Old Testament book Leviticus, 16:2, "And the Lord said to Moses: 'Tell your brother Aaron that he is not to come whenever he chooses into the Most Holy Place behind the curtain in front of the atonement cover on the ark, or else he will die. For I will appear in the cloud over the atonement cover'", (New International Version).

10. This occurred on Yom Kippur, the Day of Atonement, culminating ten days of purification rites and prayers.

11. For the full dream, see the Prologue "Note to the Reader".

12. My thanks to Sarah Young, the Chair of Help during the time of my work there and a dear friend for many years more. Thank you, too, to her husband, Martin Young, for giving so generously in more ways than one.

13. Created by the British author Ian Fleming in 1953.

14. Written by Frank Baum in 1900.

15. Attributed to John Bradshaw, an author and therapist.

16. I have shared part of this dream in *Lucid Surrender* for a different purpose.

17. "Black Lace Light II".

18. *The Hidden Lives of Dreams: What They Can Tell Us and How They Can Change Our World* (Bonnier Books, UK 2019) and *Lucid Surrender* (Archive Publishing, UK 2021).

19. The tree was toppled by a windstorm in 1969.

20. 1 John: 4:18, International Standard Version.

21. Chapter Twelve of Lucid Surrender explores the topic of "Wormholes in the Lucid Void", including their structure and purpose.

22. The idea of "greening" derives from Hildegard von Bingen's favorite theme of "O nobilissima viriditas" or "Oh most noble greenness", a theme she celebrated in her "Responsory for them Virgin". See Hildegard von Bingen, *Mystical Visions*, translated from Scivias by Bruce Hozeski and introduced by Matthew Fox (Santa Fe, NM: Bear & Company, 1995), 380. For the musical rendition of this piece, see http://www.hildegard-society.org/2017/04/ o-nobilissi-

ma-viriditas-responsory.html or *O nobilissima viriditas: The Complete Hildegard von Bingen*, Vol. 3, Peter Wishart Symphony.

23. See John 4: 1-26.

24. Based on the Old Testament scripture Isaiah 40:1.

25. *See Alice in Wonderland: The Original 1865 Edition with Complete Illustrations by Sir John Tenniel (A Classic Novel by Lewis Carroll).*

26. Paraphrased from Rainer's Rilke Second Elegy Rilke, R. M. *The Duino Elegies*, translated by H. Behn (Mount Vernon, NY: Peter Pauper Press, 1957), 7-10

27. Exodus Chapters 3 and 4, New International Version. In this Old Testament teaching, God speaks out of the burning bush to give Moses a new spiritual calling — to lead the Israelites out of Egypt.

28. My response to this dream anecdotally supports research by Rosalind Cartwright suggesting that, over time, REM dreaming of a specific emotional trauma such as divorce can help to resolve the feelings associated with the waking life event. See Rosalind D. Cartwright's early research in this area, "Dreams that Work: The Relation of Dream Incorporation to Adaptation to Stressful Events", *Dreaming*, 1, No. 1 (1991): 3–9. https://doi.org/10.1037/h0094312, and her comprehensive *The Twenty-Four Hour Mind: The Role of Sleep and Dreaming in Our Emotional Lives* (London: Oxford University Press, 2010), 162–168.

29. To learn more about IASD see https://www.asdreams.org

30. Dr Andrew Powell: *The Ways of the Soul. A Psychiatrist reflects: Essays on Life, Death and Beyond* (Aeon Books, 2020) and *Conversations with the Soul. A Psychiatrist reflects: Essays on Life, Death and Beyond* (Muswell Hill Press, 2018).

31. Published respectively in March 2019 and December 2021.

www.ingramcontent.com/pod-product-compliance
Lightning Source LLC
Chambersburg PA
CBHW040318170426
43197CB00021B/2949